A History of
AMARGOSA VALLEY,
NEVADA

A History of
AMARGOSA VALLEY, NEVADA

Robert D. McCracken

Good Luck!
Robert M. Cracken

Nye County Press

TONOPAH NEVADA

A History of Amargosa Valley, Nevada
by Robert D. McCracken

© Copyright 1990 by Nye County Press

Published in 1990 by Nye County Press
P.O. Box 3070
Tonopah, Nevada 89049

Library of Congress Catalog Card Number: 90-060813
ISBN: 1-878138-56-1
Designed by Paul Cirac, White Sage Studios, Virginia City, Nevada
Printed in the United States of America

or my daughter, Bambi

n appreciation for their unwavering support and encouragement for the Nye County Town History Project:

Nye County Commissioners

> Robert "Bobby" N. Revert
> Joe S. Garcia, Jr.
> Richard L. Carver
> Barbara J. Raper

and Nye County Planning Consultant

> Stephen T. Bradhurst, Jr.

Contents

Preface		*ix*
Acknowledgments		*xv*
1	**Prologue: The Land and Early Inhabitants**	1
	The Physical Setting	1
	Amargosa Valley's Singing Sand Dune	3
	The First Occupants	4
2	**Early Exploration**	9
	The Death Valley of the Forty-Niners	10
	In the Wake of the Forty-Niners	18
3	**Early Settlers**	27
	Cattle and Crops	27
	Longstreet: Legendary Settler	30
4	**Life in the Amargosa Valley in the 1880s**	33
	A Buckboard Journey Across the Amargosa	33
	The Frontier Home of Aaron and Rosie Winters	36
	The Discovery of Borax in Death Valley	38
5	**The Railroads Come to the Amargosa Valley**	41
	Clark Builds the LV&T	41
	Smith Builds the T&T	43
6	**People and Places — The Early 1900s**	47
	"Dad" Fairbanks	47
	Outlaw Country	56
	The Ash Meadows Clay Camps	58
	Life in Clay Camp	60

7   **The Amargosa Valley in the 1930s-1950s**   65
      Stops on the T&T Railroad   65
      The T&T Ranch–The Leeland Water & Land Company 67
      Ash Meadows During the 1930s-1950s   70
      Lathrop Wells, 1930-1950   72
      Carrara and the Marble Quarry   73
8   **Modern Development of the Amargosa Valley**   75
      Gordon and Billie Bettles on the T&T Ranch   75
      Modern Pioneers: The Records Brothers   78
      Modern Pioneer Hardships   80
      Electricity in the Amargosa Valley   84
      Law Enforcement in the Amargosa Valley   87
      Modern Mining of Amargosa Valley Clays   88
      American Borate Company in the Amargosa Valley 91
      Peat Mining the Carson Slough   93
      The Spring Meadows Ranch
         and the Pupfish Controversy   93
      Atomic Testing at the Nevada Test Site   98
      Adjusting to Life in the Amargosa Valley   99
      Growth of a Community and Its Government   101
      Amargosa Becomes an Unincorporated Town   107
9   **The Future**   109

      References   111
      Index   117

Preface

istorians generally consider the year 1890 as the close of the American frontier. By then, most of the western United States had been settled, ranches and farms developed, communities established, and roads and railroads constructed. The mining boomtowns, based on the lure of the overnight riches from newly developed lodes, were but a memory.

Although Nevada was granted statehood in 1864, examination of any map of the state from the late 1800s shows that although much of the state was mapped and its geographical features named, a vast region—stretching from Belmont south to the Las Vegas meadows, comprising most of Nye County—remained largely unsettled and unmapped. In 1890 most of southcentral Nevada, including the Amargosa Valley—or the Amargosa Desert, as it was usually known—remained very much a frontier, and it continued to be so for at least another twenty years.

The great mining booms at Tonopah (1900), Goldfield (1902), and Rhyolite (1904) represent the last major flowerings of what might be called the Old West. Aside from the Cana-

dian explorer Peter Skene Ogden, who might have set eyes on
the Amargosa Valley during his 1829–1830 expedition, the
first documented entry into the valley by whites was not until
late 1849, when the forty-niners, who had become lost in an
effort to find a shortcut to southern California, crossed the
Amargosa prior to wandering into Death Valley. The first
community, if it can be called that, was not founded in the
Amargosa until after 1905, when Ralph Jacobus "Dad" Fairbanks established his freighting and mercantile business at
the Ash Meadows spring that bears his name. The first railroad tracks did not cross the Amargosa Valley until 1906; and
from the entry of the first whites until the late 1930s, the Nye
County sheriff is said to have been hesitant to enter Ash
Meadows because of its lawless reputation. The modern
development of the Amargosa Valley by its modern pioneers
did not begin until the early 1950s. Electric power, other than
that produced by home generators, was not available until
1963. As a consequence, southcentral Nevada, notably Nye
County—perhaps more than any other region of the West—
remains close to the American frontier. In a real sense, a
significant part of the frontier can still be found there. It exists
in the attitudes, values, lifestyles, and memories of area residents. The frontier-like character of the area is also visible in
the relatively undisturbed condition of the natural environment, most of it essentially untouched by humans.

Aware of Nye County's close ties to our nation's frontier
past and the scarcity of written sources on local history
(especially after 1920), the Nye County Board of Commissioners initiated the Nye County Town History Project (NCTHP)
in 1987. The NCTHP is an effort to systematically collect and
preserve the history of Nye County. The centerpiece of the
NCTHP is a large set of interviews conducted with individuals who had knowledge of local history. The interviews provide a composite view of community and county history,

revealing the flow of life and events for a part of Nevada that has heretofore been largely neglected by historians. Each interview was recorded, transcribed, and then edited lightly, preserving the language and speech patterns of those interviewed. All oral history interviews have been printed on acid-free paper and bound and archived in Nye County libraries, Special Collections in the James R. Dickinson Library at the University of Nevada, Las Vegas, and at other archival sites located throughout Nevada.

Collection of the oral histories has been accompanied by the assembling of a set of photographs depicting each community's history. These pictures have been obtained from participants in the oral history interviews and other present and past Nye County residents. Complete sets of these photographs have been archived along with the oral histories.

The oral histories and photo collections, as well as written sources, served as the basis for the preparation of this volume on the history of Amargosa Valley. It is one of a series on the history of all major Nye County communities.

In a real sense this volume, like the others in the NCTHP series, is the result of a community effort. Before the oral interviews were conducted, a number of local residents provided advice on which community members had lived in the area the longest, possessed and recalled information not available to others, and were available and willing to participate. Because of time and budgetary constraints, many highly qualified persons were not interviewed.

Following the interviews, the participants gave even more of their time and energy: They elaborated upon and clarified points made during the taped interviews; they went through family albums and identified photographs; and they located books, dates, family records, and so forth. During the preparation of this manuscript, a number of community members were contacted, sometimes repeatedly (if asked, some would probably readily admit that they felt pestered), to answer questions that arose during the writing and editing of the manuscript. Moreover, once the manuscript was in more or less final form, each individual who was discussed for more than a paragraph or two in the text was provided with a copy of his or her portion of the text and was asked to check that portion for errors. Appropriate changes were then made in the manuscript.

Once that stage was completed, several individuals in the Amargosa Valley area were asked to review the entire manuscript for errors of omission and commission. At each stage, this quality-control process resulted in the elimination of factual errors and raised our confidence in the validity of the contents.

The author's training as an anthropologist, not a historian (although the difference between the disciplines is probably less than some might suppose), likely has something to do with the community approach taken in the preparation of this volume. It also may contribute to the focus on the details of individuals and their families as opposed to a general description of local residents and their communities. Perhaps this volume, as well as a concern with variability among individuals and their contribution to a community, reflects an "ethnographic," as opposed to a "historical," perspective on local history. In the author's view, there is no such thing as "the history" of a community; there are many histories of a community. A community's history is like a sunrise — the colors are determined by a multitude of factors, such as the time of year, weather, and point of view. This history of Amargosa Valley was greatly determined by the input of those who helped produce it. If others had participated, both the subjects treated and the relative emphasis the subjects received would have been, at least, somewhat different. Many basic facts would, of course, remain much the same — such things as names, dates, and locations of events. But the focus, the details illustrating how facts and human beings come together, would have been different. History is, and always will remain, sensitive to perspective and impressionistic, in the finest and most beautiful sense of the word.

A shorter, generously illustrated (with more than 65 photographs) companion to this volume, titled *The Modern Pioneers of the Amargosa Valley*, is also available through Nye County Press. Virtually all written material presented in that volume is contained in this one. Those who would like to see pictures of Amargosa Valley's history should consult that version.

I hope that readers enjoy this history of Amargosa Valley. True to their heritage, Amargosa's residents possess the frontier's warmth and friendliness, free of pretention. They reside in an incomparably beautiful valley that presents magnificent vistas of desert, mountains, and sky and offers a rare sense of peace and solitude. The natural world and the people in it are properly conjoined in the Amargosa Valley.

Robert D. McCracken

Acknowledgments

his volume was produced under the Nye County Town History Project, initiated by the Nye County Board of Commissioners. Appreciation goes to Chairman Joe S. Garcia, Jr., Robert "Bobby" N. Revert, and Pat Mankins; Mr. Revert and Mr. Garcia, in particular, showed deep interest and unyielding support for the project from its inception. Thanks also go to current commissioners Richard L. Carver and Barbara J. Raper, who have since joined Mr. Revert on the board and who have continued the project with enthusiastic support. Stephen T. Bradhurst, Jr., planning consultant for Nye County, gave unwavering support and advocacy, provided advice and input regarding the conduct of the research, and constantly served as a sounding board as production problems were worked out. This volume would never have been possible without the enthusiastic support of the Nye County commissioners and Mr. Bradhurst.

Thanks go to the participants of the Nye County Town History Project, especially those from the Amargosa Valley and the Amargosa area, who kindly provided much of the information; thanks, also, to residents from Amargosa Valley and throughout southern Nevada—too numerous to mention by name—who provided assistance and historical information.

Jean Charney and Jean Stoess did the word processing and, along with Gary Roberts, Maire Hayes, and Jodie Hansen, provided editorial comments, review, and suggestions. Alice Levine and Michelle Starika edited several drafts of the manuscript and contributed measurably to this volume's scholarship and readability. Alice Levine also served as production consultant, and Michelle Starika prepared the index. Paul Cirac, who was raised in central Nevada, was responsible for design and layout. Gretchen Loeffler and Bambi McCracken assisted in numerous secretarial and clerical duties. Doris Jackson, Hank Records, Betty-Jo Boyd, Deke Lowe, and Celesta Lowe kindly critiqued several drafts of the manuscript; their assistance and support have been invaluable. Kevin Rafferty and Lynda Blair, from the University of Nevada, Las Vegas, Environmental Research Center, provided helpful suggestions on the section concerning the archaeology of Native Americans in the Amargosa Valley area. Phillip Earl of the Nevada Historical Society contributed valuable support and criticism throughout, and Tom King at the Oral History Program of the University of Nevada, Reno, served as consulting oral historian. Susan Jarvis and Kathy War of Special Collections, James R. Dickinson Library, University of Nevada, Las Vegas, assisted greatly with research conducted at that institution. Much deserved thanks are extended to all these persons.

All aspects of production of this volume were supported

by the U.S. Department of Energy, Grant No. DE-FG08-89NV10820. However, any opinions, findings, conclusions, or recommendations expressed herein are those of the author and do not necessarily reflect the views of DOE. Any errors or deficiencies are, of course, the author's responsibility.

R. D. M.

CHAPTER 1

Prologue: The Land
and Early Inhabitants

he Amargosa Valley did not yield itself easily to human habitation. Although it is not as famous (or notorious) as Death Valley, its immediate neighbor to the west, the Amargosa is formidable enough. Rainfall is scarce, and vegetation is sparse; most of the valley is arid and treeless. This volume describes some of the efforts of the hearty individuals who have succeeded in making the valley their home.

The Physical Setting

The Amargosa Valley is the broad, flat valley lying mostly south, but in some locations a little north, of U.S. Highway 95 between Beatty and a point a few miles west of Mercury in southern Nye County, Nevada. In his classic volume *Place Names of the Death Valley Region in California and Nevada*, T. S. Palmer (1980:6) defined the Amargosa Desert, now known as the Amargosa Valley, as "the wide valley extending from the Bullfrog Hills to the south end of Shoshone Lake Flats, between Ibex Hills and Kingston Mountains." Julian Steward,

1

writing in the 1930s, stated, "The great Amargosa Desert, lying east of Death Valley, is some 40 miles long, 12 and more miles wide, only 2,500 to 3,000 feet above sea level, and almost devoid of water and edible plants" (1970:93).

The term Amargosa comes from the Spanish word *amargroso*, which means "bitter" and refers to the quality of the water in the Amargosa River. The Amargosa River begins 10 miles north of Beatty at Springdale, taking its water from springs, and flows beneath the surface southeastward across the Amargosa Valley "to the California line, where it turns northwest and becomes lost in Death Valley" (Carlson, 1974:36). The Amargosa has been variously known as Alkali Creek, The Bitter Water, Bitter Water Creek, Salaratus Creek, Amargoshe Creek, and Anorgosa (Carlson, 1974:36-37). There are no permanent lakes in the Amargosa Valley, and, as Helen Carlson wrote (1974:37), it is "almost destitute of vegetation except for grass growing near a few springs." The exception is Ash Meadows, a verdant area in the southeast portion of the valley featuring meadows and springs, "so named for the leather-leaved ash trees which grow in abundance there" (Carlson, 1974:41-42). Another source states the name Ash Meadows can be attributed to the ashy color of the alkaline soil (Cook and Williams, 1982:IV-1). Ash Meadows, which is approximately 63 square miles (Cook and Williams, 1982:I-1), has elevation ranges between 2120 and 2800 feet above sea level. More than 20 major springs discharge an average of 17,000 acre-feet of mineral-rich water annually, creating a "natural desert oasis unsurpassed by any in the American Southwest" (Cook and Williams, 1982:I-1). Water from these springs is said to originate in the deep, carboniferous aquifer that underlies much of eastern and southern Nevada and western Utah (Bradhurst, 1987). Most of the water discharged in Ash Meadows is believed to be "fossil water" deposited by a system of interconnecting lakes prior to 10,000 years ago (Cook and Williams, 1982:III-4). In the Amargosa Valley farm area, by contrast, the wells draw water that is of surface origin, draining a large area to the northeast of the valley (Bradhurst, 1987). Ash Meadows, which has also been known as Ash Meadow Valley and Meadow Valley (Carlson, 1974:41-42), is drained by the Carson Slough, a tributary of the Amargosa River.

Amargosa Valley's Singing Sand Dune

For centuries people in the Middle East and in China have noted that some desert sand dunes emit acoustical energy (sound) when disturbed. The phenomenon has been described variously as roaring, booming, squeaking, singing, or resembling one of several musical instruments (kettle drum, zither, tambourine, bass violin, or trumpet). Other descriptions liken the sound to a foghorn or a low-flying, propeller-driven aircraft (Trexler and Melhorn, 1986:147).

Most desert dunes do not emit sound; only about thirty around the world are known to do so. And those that do, do not sing on all occasions. Dune sound emissions are not well understood, but they appear to be connected to the "mechanical coupling between grains" when sands avalanche down a dune slope. The initial sound, which is produced by the grains abrading on each other, becomes a lower audio frequency that is then amplified. In some instances an observer can feel the vibrations when a dune sings (Trexler and Melhorn, 1986:148).

Three singing dunes are known in Nevada: one at Sand Mountain 18 miles southeast of Fallon; Crescent Dunes about 10 miles northeast of Tonopah; and Big Dune in the Amargosa Valley.

Big Dune lies in the northern part of the Amargosa Valley, about 10 miles south of Beatty and 5.5 miles northeast of the

Nevada-California state line. It is clearly visible in the distance to the southwest from U.S. Highway 95. Big Dune's crest is approximately 300 feet above the valley floor. It is reached by turning south off Highway 95 at the Amargosa Farm sign, proceeding 2.5 miles, then west on the dirt road in the direction of the dune. In 1985 the photogenic beauty of Big Dune provided the backdrop for scenes in which Las Vegas Strip casinos were buried in desert sands in the futuristic movie *Cherry 2000*.

The First Occupants

We do not know when humans first entered the Amargosa Valley. Ancient campsites testify to occupation of Death Valley by human beings at least 10,000 years ago, after the end of the last Ice Age (Lingenfelter, 1986:16). Recent examination of archaeological remains in the Amargosa Valley implies more extensive use by aborigines than had been previously estimated. Remains show interesting relationships to adjoining areas and peoples, with possible long-term occupation. Pottery remains dating from around A.D. 1000 to historic times have been found. They indicate seasonal use of the Amargosa Valley by semisedentary hunters and gatherers, as well as more nomadic groups (Brooks and Larson, 1973:10; Blair, 1989). There are also the pottery remains of Virgin Anasazi groups from eastern Clark County at a few sites dating A.D. 500 to 1200 (Rafferty, 1989).

During the nineteenth century, two groups of American Indians occupied the Amargosa Valley: the Western Shoshone and the Southern Paiute. Both groups practiced economies based on the collection of wild plant foods supplemented by the hunting of game. Both were extremely adept at extracting a living from a marginal environment. A number of groups, or camps, of Southern Paiute lived in southern Nevada during this period, including populations at Indian Springs, Potosi, Pa-room Spring (probably Pahrump Spring), Las Vegas, Cottonwood Island, Kingston Mountain [Peak], Ivanpah, and Providence Mountain. Camps of Southern Paiute were also located at Ash Meadows and on the Amargosa River (Steward, 1970:181-182). During the latter part of the nineteenth century, the Southern Paiute living at Ash Meadows numbered about 31 and were known as the Kau-yai'-chits. Their leader was Nu-a'-rung. Those living at Amargosa numbered about 68 and were known as the Ya'gats. Their leader was Ni-a-pa'-ga-rats. Both populations were probably mixed with Shoshone. The total population of all the Las Vegas-area Southern Paiute camps listed above probably numbered less than 450 (computed from Steward, 1970:182).

The greatest asset of the Southern Paiute living in the Ash Meadows Valley was the Spring Mountains to the east, which rise to a height of 11,910 feet at Charleston Peak. The mountains afforded abundant pine nuts, seeds, and considerable game (Steward, 1970:182). Pine nut tracts were owned by men and inherited by their sons; women gathered on their husbands' land (Steward, 1970:183). Though there were sometimes disputes regarding ownership of tracts, permission to gather was always granted to families who owned tracts where crops had failed. Cones were pulled from trees with poles 15 to 20 feet long with hooks on their ends. When the Spring Mountains crops failed, the Paiute picked in the Shoshone Mountains. Mesquite grew in abundance at Ash Meadows, and beans were picked in family-owned groves; screw beans were another important food source in Ash Meadows. These Paiute also picked sand bunch grass seeds at the Calico Hills and at the Big Dune, where sometimes Beatty Shoshone were encountered. They also collected foods in the Funeral Mountains and near Cane Spring (Steward, 1970:183).

The Ash Meadows Paiute, like their neighbors in Pahrump Valley, also practiced aboriginal horticulture. They grew corn, squash, beans, and sunflowers in small fields in moist soil near streams. Families without land traded wild plants and foods for cultivated crops. Crops in the field were destroyed when the owner died, even if harvest was near. Cultivated and wild foods were never abundant enough to allow permanent settlement in the area (Steward, 1970:183).

Hunting played a relatively minor role in Southern Paiute survival. The Ash Meadows Paiute hunted deer in the Spring Mountains, where they dried the meat and skins and carried their take home in nets. Mountain sheep, which were abundant at that time, could be found in the Funeral Mountains and in the mountains between the Amargosa River and Pahrump Valley. Deer and sheep were hunted both by individuals and by groups of men without leaders or formal organization. It was customary, even obligatory, for the hunter to share large game with his neighbors (Steward, 1970:182-184).

The outstanding group activity that united area residents was the annual fall festival. Members of several small groups or encampments attended. Visitors would come from Beatty, Ash Meadows, Pahrump Valley, Las Vegas, and even from San Bernardino. The festival was planned months in advance and was directed by the local "chief." The chief made speeches and the people danced, often at the same time. The festival lasted three or four days and on the last night, buckskins and other items were burned for those who had died within the year. The last festival was held shortly after the turn of the century. This festival was the only important communal activity of the Southern Paiute (Steward, 1970:184).

Warfare was probably not important for the Ash Meadows Paiute. Chiefs had little authority outside their own small groups, which were composed of extended family members.

Chief Tecopa, who was born in Las Vegas, was named a chief of the Ash Meadows and Pahrump groups. Tecopa, who died in 1904, was considered by many to be the chief of all Southern Paiute, but he had no functions aside from directing the festival and transactions with white men (Steward, 1970:185). The Southern Paiute, unlike their neighbors, the Western Ute, never adopted the horse for transportation, preferring to use the beasts for food (Steward, 1970:181).

The Western Shoshone, with whom the Ash Meadows and Amargosa Paiute mixed, occupied a vast region encompassing northwestern Utah and all of northeastern and most of central Nevada, as well as territory extending into Owens and Death valleys (see map, D'Azevedo, 1986:IX). In the Amargosa Valley region the Western Shoshone occupied "the northern halves of Death Valley and Panamint Valley, all of Saline Valley, the southern end of Eureka Valley, the southern shores of Owens Lake, and Koso Mountain region, the northern edge of the Mojave Desert, and the eastern slope of the Sierra Nevada Mountains" (Steward, 1970:71). The Shoshone occupied the Beatty and Belted Mountains areas; in 1875 the population of Beatty was 29 and 42 lived in the Belted Mountains (Steward, 1970:48). The Southern Paiute at Ash Meadows called themselves Nu. Shoshone located there were called Koyohuts, or Kwoiaxo'tza, by other Shoshone (Steward, 1970:71). Most of the year, the Indian families pursued subsistence independently. A family usually wintered in the same area year after year. The variety of terrain roamed by the Shoshone in this area is probably greater than any other area of equal size in North America, ranging from Death Valley to elevations high in the Panamint Mountains and Sierra Nevada (Steward, 1970:72).

The main food sources were vegetable, with the most important being pine nuts. Most pine nut plots were not

owned by individual Shoshone, in contrast with Paiute practice. In good years, enough pine nuts could be gathered in a
few weeks, or at most two months, to last most of the winter.
In the spring, when food supplies became exhausted, families
would usually leave their winter villages to seek out the first
greens of spring and to hunt antelope and rabbits. During the
summer, small groups would move into areas where various
seeds ripened at different times. Journeys into the mountains
also afforded the opportunity to escape the summer heat of
the valleys. Gathered seeds were considered private property,
and women shared them with their husbands, children, and
parents, and presented gifts of food on occasion to siblings
and other relatives. Large game was shared communally in
the village (Steward, 1970:72-74).

Like the Southern Paiute, the Shoshone held a fall festival,
which included the circle dance, gambling, and annual
mourning observances. The festival enlisted people from considerable territory and they participated with great enthusi-
asm. The direction of the fall festival was the most important
task of the chief (Steward, 1970:74-75).

There were few political controls on individuals, with
behavior being governed more by individuals' involvement
within family units. Intervillage alliances were temporary
and shifting. Often, one village would associate with another
village more than with others, and areas embracing such
associations were known as districts (Steward, 1970:74-75).

CHAPTER 2

Early Exploration

outhcentral Nevada, a vast region broken by desert valleys and divided by mountain ranges, remained relatively unexplored until the 1850s. Jedediah Smith, an American fur trapper, was the first to explore the Colorado River on Nevada's southern border; he made forays into that country in 1826 and again in 1827. New Mexican merchant Antonio Armijo is credited with pioneering the cutoff from the Colorado River that led through the Las Vegas Valley and across the Pahrump Valley in 1829 (Warren, 1974). This route, a portion of the Old Spanish Trail, enjoyed extensive use between 1830 and about 1848 (Reeder, 1966:8). After 1848 the route from Los Angeles to Santa Fe fell into disuse and the Las Vegas portion became part of what was known as the Mormon Trail, joining Salt Lake City with southern California.

It is possible, though not highly likely (Roske, 1986), that Canadian trapper and explorer Peter Skene Ogden passed through the Amargosa Valley as he traveled south through southcentral Nevada in his Snake Country Expedition of

1829-1830 (Cline, 1974:93). In the spring of 1844, John C. Fremont, on his second expedition, passed through the Pahrump Valley and the Las Vegas Meadows on his way east. Fremont published a map of the Great Basin in 1848, which featured a substantial—though, as we now know, nonexistent—mountain range running east and west across the Great Basin in the vicinity of present-day Beatty. Fremont based his map on information gathered on his third expedition in 1845-1846, when his party passed north of Beatty in the Toiyabe Range area.

Horse thieves were also important in the early exploration of the Amargosa Valley. Starting in 1832 and 1833, various thieves began driving stolen herds out of California along a route that took them over Tehachapi Pass, then along the rift of the Gerlock Fault from the foot of the Sierra to the south end of Death Valley; they would link up with the Spanish Trail at Salt Spring. Lingenfelter (1986:26) stated, "This route was much used by later horse thieves and came to be known as 'Walker's cutoff,' either because it ran to Walker Pass or because it was frequented by the Ute raider Walkara, called Walker by the whites. This was the highly touted shortcut that the argonauts were seeking when they blundered into Death Valley in 1849."

The Death Valley of the Forty-Niners

The saga of the forty-niners' troubles in Death Valley is one of the best-known, dramatic, and heroic tales in the history of the American West. It begins with the discovery of gold in California at Sutter's Mill on the American River on January 24, 1848. Prior to 1849, approximately 15,000 people had migrated to California and Oregon by the transcontinental route. Another 4600, mostly Mormons, had settled in the Salt Lake Valley. In contrast, an estimated 25,000 people migrated overland to California in 1849, the first year of the Gold Rush (Johnson, 1987:3).

During the late summer and fall of 1849 a number of California-bound travelers arrived in Salt Lake City. They were well aware of the dangers of crossing the Sierra Nevada late in the season and were encouraged by the Mormons to travel south from Salt Lake City to a point where they could join the Old Spanish Trail, which would lead them safely to Los Angeles. They were advised that they could then travel north through California to the gold fields. The advantages of the southern route were a minimum of snow and no major mountain ranges to cross (Johnson, 1987:3).

The travelers accepted the Mormons' advice and hired as a guide Jefferson Hunt, a former captain of the Mormon Battalion in the Mexican War. Hunt had traversed the trail in the winter of 1847-1848. He charged a fee of $10 per wagon. In early October 1849 Hunt led a wagon train, consisting of more than 100 wagons and roughly 1000 oxen, cattle, and pack animals, south from Hobble Creek, south of Provo, Utah (Johnson, 1987:3).

After the wagons had been on the trail for about two weeks, they were overtaken by a party of packers led by a 20-year-old New Yorker, Captain Orson K. Smith (Lingenfelter, 1986:34). Smith was in possession of a map, which, it was said, would cut 300 to 500 miles off the trip to the California gold fields. The map is believed to have been a print of Fremont's 1848 map of the Great Basin, with some additions made by a mountain man named Williams and information supplied by the "celebrated chief of the Ute horsethieves, Walkara" (Belden, 1956:22-23). Walkara is reported to have originally drawn the "map" of his shortcut in the sand with a stick (Belden, 1956:23). Though Walkara's shortcut showed a fork from the Spanish Trail near the present site of Tecopa, Califor-

nia, Smith's map began the shortcut near Cedar City, Utah
(Belden, 1956:23). Fremont's map incorrectly showed a mountain range extending west, creating a southern boundary to
the Great Basin (Johnson, 1987:53). Fremont's map also la-
beled the area "unexplored" (Johnson, 1987:4). Dissention
arose among the travelers: stay with Jefferson Hunt as agreed
or follow Captain Smith and his map. They were in a hurry to
reach California, so the vast majority elected to go with Smith.
As they left, Jefferson Hunt warned them, "If you want to
follow Captain Smith, I can't help it, but I believe you will get
into the jaws of hell" (Lingenfelter, 1986:39).

Those travelers who elected to stay with Hunt or eventually returned to his route arrived safely in due time in southern California. Those who chose to go with Smith and stayed
with him did, indeed, go "into the jaws of hell." Traveling only
with pack animals, Smith quickly left his followers and their
wagons behind. Those who continued soon broke into small
groups seeking different routes across the unknown wastes of
Nevada. One such group was the Jayhawkers, approximately
3 dozen men, mostly from Knoxville and Galesburg, Illinois,
with a dozen wagons between them. Another was the
Bugsmashers, approximately a dozen men, including 3 blacks,
mostly from Georgia and Mississippi, with about a half-dozen
wagons. There were a number of families, including those of
Asabell Bennett, John Arcan, Harry Wade, and the Reverend
James Brier (Lingenfelter, 1986:40). In all, over 80 men, 4
women, 11 children, more than 2 dozen wagons, and over 100
oxen continued on the so-called shortcut (Lingenfelter, 1986:40).

The travelers who stayed with Hunt followed a course
that roughly parallels Interstate Highway 15. Those who were
led astray by Smith's 1848 Fremont map headed due west
from near the site of Enterprise, Utah (Johnson, 1987:53). After
three days of easy travel up Shoal Creek, those who had split

off from Hunt encountered Beaver Dam Wash and a long, deep chasm, which became known as Mount Misery, that stopped the oxen. With his pack animals, Smith was able to find a way around, but the others were not. About 75 wagons turned back at Mount Misery to follow Hunt. Those who stayed found a detour and continued west. The going was difficult and those who remained broke into smaller and smaller groups. Near Papoose Dry Lake, in southwestern Nevada, the Bugsmashers, the Jayhawkers, and the Brier family headed due west, while another group of at least 7 wagons, the Bennett-Arcan group, turned south (Johnson, 1987:4). All parties eventually wound up in the Amargosa Valley on their way to Death Valley, thus becoming the first white and black people known to have set foot in the valley. The route followed by the forty-niners across the Amargosa and into Death Valley has been the subject of considerable investigation by modern researchers. Leroy and Jean Johnson, two such researchers, wrote that the Bennett-Arcan families, William L. Manly, John H. Rogers, and their drivers

> crossed the Amargosa Desert (49 miles southeast of Beatty, west of Highway 95) in the company of at least three other wagons and entered the east side of Ash Meadows near Devils Hole. After camping at Collins Spring, where they found firewood, grass, and water less than a mile south of Devils Hole, they headed almost due west through the brackish sloughs in Ash Meadows, crossed the Amargosa riverbed, and ascended the slope of the Funeral Mountains about where Highway 190 makes its way west from Death Valley Junction.... They descended the western flank of the Funeral Mountains through Furnace Creek Wash to Travertine Springs 3.5 miles east of where Furnace Creek Inn now stands (Johnson, 1987:38).

The Bennett-Arcan wagon train entered Ash Meadows from the east through a low pass in the hills and followed an Indian trail southwesterly to Devils Hole and Indian occupation sites nearby. The trail, paralleling the current dirt road, leads to Devils Hole, a small pool hidden 50 feet down in a fault fissure at the base of a limestone hill ... the immigrants stopped at Devils Hole since it was the first water they had encountered in many miles (Johnson, 1987:55).

Nearly 40 years later, in 1888, William L. Manly described Ash Meadows from memory:

We now started on again. On the second or third night we camped near a hole of clear water [Devils Hole, Ash Meadows, Nevada] which was quite deep and had some little minus [minnows] in. Grass was good and plenty for our cattle. The next day we crossed a shallow stream of peculiar tasting water [in Carson Slough]. It seemed to be medicated in some way by the way in which it acted on those who drank much of it. I think it came from a mine of salts.

Here we came in the road of those who had gone and left us. The path led up hill and it looked like a very long pull [near highway from Death Valley Junction westward]. I went ahead until I could see that the road was a very long one with no prospects for water. I then turned back to see if our party had filled their kegs with water. I found they had not. I told them they might have to go forty miles without the way the country looked. They then unloaded the lightest wagon and went back for water (Johnson, 1987:55-56; information in brackets from Johnson).

The Johnsons (1987:56) stated that the water kegs were not initially filled with water, so that the weakened oxen could more easily pull the lighter wagons through the Carson Slough, which one forty-niner described as "horrible alkali marshes."

Because the Ash Meadows area has numerous springs, the parties probably assumed that they could find water along the trail ahead of them. Manly recalled:

> I then pushed on and near the summit I found a dead ox. Someone had cut a big gash square across the ham and it had dried. I cut a big slice from it and ate as I went along. I was hungry and it tasted very good. I turned the summit and pushed down the canyon [Furnace Creek Wash] and found a little water on the face of a clay bluff in a hole that held about a quart. I got a good drink and passed on. The canyon, as well as the whole range was barren, dry and very volcanic. It was now a heavy downgrade, but not rocky. No more water was found till near the mouth of the canyon. I walked down the lonesome dry bottom and about an hour after dark came to Mr. Brier's camp, where there were numerous weak springs and a little grass [Travertine Springs] (Johnson, 1987:56).

Louis Nusbaumer, a German immigrant and member of the Bennett-Arcan party, kept a diary in which he described his travels across southern Nevada. His entry for 12-23-1849 described Ash Meadows.

> We arrive at a beautiful valley [Ash Meadows] considerably lower than we had been before and quite a warm region so that we encountered flies, butterflies, beetles, etc. At the entrance to the valley to the right is a hole in the rocks [Devils Hole] which contains magnificent warm water and in which Hadapp and I enjoyed an extremely refreshing bath. The temperature of the water is about 24-26° [75-79°F] and the saline cavity itself presents a magical appearance. It seems the Christ child will show us the right way. # (24th) Our prospects begin to become more dismal again, since one of our oxen is about to die, though we will not lose courage

on the eve of the day on which our Savior was born (Johnson, 1987:161, including bracketed information).

The Jayhawkers, Bugsmashers, and the Briers entered the Amargosa Valley in the vicinity of Fortymile Canyon, "a wash and a canyon extending northward from a point west of Lathrop Wells and southeast of Yucca Mountain" (Carlson, 1974:115; Johnson, 1987:172). The Briers and another group were forced to abandon their wagons in the vicinity of Forty-mile Canyon; they hiked out of its mouth and the "mountains ahead forced them south along the Amargosa riverbed until they found a path heading west—near Death Valley Junction" (Johnson, 1987:172). The Briers, the Georgian Bugsmashers, and the Jayhawkers used Furnace Creek Wash as a gateway into Death Valley, while the Mississippian Bugsmashers traveled a more northerly route, possibly Cox Creek (Belden, 1956:27). The Georgian Bugsmashers abandoned their wagons in the Amargosa Valley at a place now known as Lost Wagons (Belden, 1956:31).

Much of the trouble later encountered by the Bennett-Arcan parties in Death Valley could have been avoided. Manly, scouting ahead, climbed Mount Sterling at the northwest end of the Spring Mountains and saw smoke from campfires 30 miles to the south. Lingenfelter suggested the smoke must have been from the camps of the last straggling wagons of the Hunt train, which had turned back to the Spanish/Mormon Trail and were camped at either Stump Spring or Resting Spring at the time.

> Ironically, Manly didn't realize that after more than a month of wandering he was only two days' travel from the Spanish Trail and that relief was in sight. Instead, he concluded that the smoke was from Indian camps, so he decided that he and the families should also head west. Thus they

followed the Jayhawkers and Bugsmashers into Death Valley, but at the mouth of Furnace Creek they turned south again, away from the others and into the very sink of Death Valley, to camp at the springs west of Badwater. There, on the verge of starvation, the Bennett and Arcan families would remain for over a month (Lingenfelter, 1986:42-43).

The Bennett and Arcan parties were eventually rescued from Death Valley when William L. Manly and a companion, John H. Rogers, walked out of Death Valley into the San Fernando Valley to obtain supplies and returned to rescue their companions. This rescue is one of the great examples of courage in the American West, for to obtain help Manly and Rogers had to travel on foot over 270 miles across unknown desert lands. They could have easily abandoned the families as four wagon drivers had done earlier.

The other parties that had wandered into Death Valley found various routes out of their predicament. One Jayhawker party escaped the valley by ascending Towne Pass (Belden, 1956:36). One forty-niner, Harry Wade, found a path through Wingate Wash, pioneering the trail used by the first borax wagons from Death Valley to Daggett (Lingenfelter, 1986:48). Few realized that escape from Death Valley was possible simply by following the valley farther south instead of trying to cross the mountains to the west (Lingenfelter, 1986:51); of the two dozen wagons that left Mount Misery, the only two to make it took that route (Lingenfelter, 1986:49). On the morning of February 15, Manly, Rogers, and the Bennett and Arcan families were camped high in the Panamints just short of the crest. They had climbed a little knoll—hill 7478—beyond the pass so that they might study the route of their journey to come. On the way down, Arcan took a long look back at the valley from which he had emerged and uttered his famous farewell: "Goodbye Death Valley!" And so the valley was named (Lingenfelter, 1986:50-51; Johnson, 1987:42). Bennett and Arcan's shortcut from Mount Misery to the Los Angeles area took four months, but the forty-niners' ordeal transformed Death Valley and the Amargosa from a "lonely piece of desert into the deadliest, richest, and most mysterious spot in America" (Lingenfelter, 1986:51).

In the Wake of the Forty-Niners

The argonauts' narrow escape from Death Valley became widely known and fueled interest in the region. Tales of lost silver and gold mines added to the fire. Jim Martin, one of the Bugsmashers from the Georgia and Mississippi party, had found rich silver-lead ore in a spur of the Panamints while escaping, and later he had a specimen that he had carried out refined and made into a gunsight. As early as the 1850s his find became known as the Lost Gunsight Lode (Lingenfelter, 1986:43, 59).

Charles C. Breyfogle had come west in 1849, spent some time in California and the Comstock, and was running a hotel at Geneva, located on Birch Creek on the east side of the Toiyabe Range, in 1863. Accounts of Breyfogle's discovery vary. One version holds that years before, he had met one of the Death Valley forty-niners, who told of a vast ledge of quartz rich in gold. In 1864 Breyfogle and some companions set out to find the gold. Upon arriving at the Amargosa Valley they split up to prospect the surrounding hills. On one venture Breyfogle returned to camp after several days half-starved after having been lost. He had several specimens that were said to have later assayed as high as $4500 a ton in gold. As luck would have it, the party was out of food and had to leave. Although he returned to the area several times, Breyfogle was never able to locate the place where he originally found his rich specimen. During one trip there, in 1865, he was attacked and nearly killed by Ash Meadow Paiute as he wandered along the Amargosa River. The deposit of gold became known as the Lost Breyfogle Lode. Those looking for it were said to have gone "Breyfogling." No one knows how many man-hours and how much money were later spent looking for the Lost Gunsight and Breyfogle lodes, but they were very substantial (Lingenfelter, 1986:73-79).

Governmental and privately sponsored surveyors arrived in the Amargosa Valley region not far behind the first miners. A privately financed party was in the region in 1853 looking at the possibility of using one of the forty-niners' paths through the area as a railroad route (Lingenfelter, 1986:80). Several Mormon prospecting expeditions made their way into the Death Valley-Amargosa area between 1851 and 1858 when the route between Salt Lake City and San Bernardino was most frequented. In fact, Furnace Creek was named by Dr. E. Darwin French in 1860 because of the crude rock furnaces constructed by Mormons at that site in 1857 (Wheat, 1939:4). In the winter of 1853 Fremont headed his last expedition, intending to determine the feasibility of trains crossing the Rockies in the winter. He crossed Nevada at about the 37th parallel, just north of Beatty (Noren, 1982:7L), on a line between just south of Pioche and a little south of Bishop, California (Egan, 1985:503).

After 1861, four different survey teams passed through southern Nevada while conducting boundary surveys on the oblique border between California and the Utah-New Mexico territories, above the Colorado River (Warren, 1980:207). These surveys were led by Dr. J.R.N. Owen (who utilized camels) in 1861; Butler Ives, J. F. Houghton, and J. F. Kidder in 1863; James Lawson in 1865; and Alexis von Schmidt in 1872 and 1873 (Warren, 1980:207-208).

The Owen expedition left Fort Mojave on February 13, 1861, and after eleven days' travel, by way of the Providence Mountains, Ivanpah Dry Lake, the Potosi Mines, and Stump Spring (on the Old Spanish Trail), reached Resting Spring. After stopping there, the group moved north past the present site of the town of Tecopa, crossed to the Amargosa River near the present site of Shoshone, then proceeded to Eagle Mountain, which they called Amargosa Butte. The party then continued north in the Amargosa Valley past the site of Death Valley Junction and over the broad plain of the Amargosa Desert (Wheat, 1939:12). On March 2, they camped in the alkali beds beside the Amargosa River. Because of their padded feet, the camels that were used by the group had a great advantage over the mules on the sandy floor of the Amargosa Valley; in mountainous country the mules proved to be superior travelers.

In the Amargosa Valley, the group crossed the faint trail left by a party of forty-niners twelve years earlier as they unwisely moved toward Death Valley. Later the survey party camped near a small water hole in the eastern foothills of the Funeral Mountains, then known as the Amargosa Mountains. A dry camp was made on the desert east of the point known now as Chloride Cliff; when the guide was unable to locate water, the party was forced to retrace its steps. At one point the men ascended to the crest of the Funerals, probably at or very near Chloride Cliff. The view to the west that met their eyes from this vantage point was a sight "of extraordinarily rude and disorderly grandeur" in contrast to the "comparatively tame" country that lay to the east across the Amargosa Valley (Wheat, 1939:12-13). The party eventually descended into Death Valley, moved on to Panamint Valley and to Owens Lake (Wheat, 1939:14-15).

In 1867, the U.S. Army and the California Geological

Survey combined in a geological survey of the area between Independence, California, and Oasis Valley, Nevada (Warren, 1980:208). Lieutenant George M. Wheeler conducted geological surveys in the vicinity of the Amargosa Valley in 1871 and 1875 (Warren, 1980:209); and the U.S. Department of Agriculture sponsored a study of life forms in the Death Valley region in 1891 (Warren, 1980:210).

In the spring of 1866, Henry Goode Blasdel (the first governor of the state of Nevada) and a party that included R. H. Stretch, state mineralogist, undertook exploration in the southern part of Nevada; their chief purpose was to open a more direct line of communication between the state capital at Carson City and the new Pahranagat mining district near the southeastern border of the state. They hoped to find a more practicable route than the one through Egan Canyon and Austin (Wheat, 1939:15). Traveling southeast from Carson City the party reached Montgomery City on March 25, 1866, then turned southeast to the youthful mining community of Silver Peak. From there the party moved south through Alida Valley to Desert Springs, Bonner Springs, and on to Wilson's Well at the extreme northern reaches of Death Valley. Moving south through Death Valley, the party encountered Lost Wagons, the remains of the wagons that the Jayhawker party of forty-niners had burned before escaping Death Valley. Leaving Lost Wagons the party continued southeast to the site of the present National Park Service headquarters. At Furnace Creek Wash, the expedition was forced to deal with the same problem the forty-niners faced—except in reverse: how to get out of Death Valley (this time toward the east). A portion of the group (six men) attempted to find an easy way over the Funeral Mountains but missed the route up Furnace Creek Wash. About this time the legendary Charles Breyfogle showed up at the camp presumably having come down Furnace Creek

Wash. Governor Blasdel hired a wagon and a large water
cask from Breyfogle's group, and with two of Breyfogle's
companions as guides, headed up Furnace Creek Wash to aid
the six others. The men had climbed over the Funeral Mountains, descended to the Amargosa Valley, but had found no
potable water. Eventually, all but one of the party of the six
were found. The man who died (C. Gillis of Carson City,
Nevada) left camp in the Amargosa while the others retraced
their steps toward Furnace Creek. A suitable route to Pahranagat was soon found by the group. Under Governor Blasdel
the expedition crossed the Amargosa Valley and journeyed to
the Pahranagat mining district near the present towns of Hiko
and Crystal Springs, by way of Indian Springs, located about
40 miles north of the Las Vegas meadows. In mid-May the
governor and his party headed for home from the Pahranagat
district, not by way of Death and Amargosa valleys but by
way of Eureka and Austin (Wheat, 1939:16-18; James, 1989:20).

In 1867 R. H. Stretch described what he had seen in the
Amargosa Valley on that expedition.

> May 7th—We have been in camp most of the time up to
> this date. During this time, we made an unsuccessful at-
> tempt to find a pass out to the eastward. Death Valley proper
> is about thirty miles long and ten wide, the greater portion
> of its area being covered with incrustations of salt. It is ex-
> ceedingly destitute of vegetation, and surrounded by moun-
> tains of great height, though the fact of their not reaching the
> snow line attests the great depression of the valley below the
> surrounding country. This morning we broke camp. Our
> road lay through rough mountains for over twenty miles,
> the higher portions of the range being similar to those near
> Bonner Springs. The low, broken hills on each side of the
> cañon are made up of sandstone, shales, conglomerates,
> gravel beds, and mud banks on the western side of the

summits, capped with basalt on the eastern slope. The color of the formation ranges from dirty white, through yellow, yellowish brown, dark brown to black, as it recedes from the center of the cañon, imparting to the country a very peculiar appearance. The gravel beds must be many hundred feet in thickness, and have sometimes been tilted in common with the shales on which they rest, while in other places they are unconformable. The conglomerates are often seamed with veins filled with compact limestone, and cutting the formation at an obtuse angle. We came to camp on the eastern side of the valley; water and grass abundant. Amargosa Valley must be two thousand feet higher than Death Valley, and extends northward as far as Silver Peak, but its water-shed is to Death Valley, with which it is connected, along the northern margin of the great Mohave Desert. It is about twelve or fifteen miles wide, thinly covered with sage brush, and large portions of it are covered with salt grass. Water is abundant a few feet below the surface, but often poor in quality.

May 10th—Six miles across meadow and sand flats, with some small white ash timber and grape vines, brought us to a range of low coralline limestone hills, with a fine spring on the summit, in a cave thirty feet long and ten wide. Crossed Ash Creek about three miles from camp. Camped on dry flat, with water three feet below surface.

May 11th—Ten miles across desert flats to foothills; then eight miles to hard table land, with broken mountains to the summit. Shrubby cacti abundant, taking the place of the globular varieties, hitherto predominant. Mountains, limestone. On the top of a high tabular hill Mr. White found a profusion of fossil shells, chiefly large conical univalves. It is to be regretted that the specimens collected have been lost on their way to Carson. Indian tracks abundant on the summit, which, to the south rises into the lofty snow range known as the Spring Mountains. Still following the general easterly course which we have maintained since leaving Death Valley, thirteen miles brought us to Indian Springs. Water and grass scarce. Few small mesquite bushes; no other timber seen to-day (Stretch, 1867:144-145).

Stretch summarized the features of the country that they had traversed:

> parallelism of mountain ranges ... alternation with these mountains of wide valleys, sometime covered with sage brush, but often containing wide mud flats as completely destitute of vegetation as the floor of a room.... A complete absence of timber, the only wood being small mesquite brushes near the springs ... scarcity of water ... prevalence of wide gravel washes at the mouth of cañons ... scarcity of Indians through the district (Stretch, 1867:145-146).

Second Lieutenant D.A. Lyle was a member of Lieutenant George M. Wheeler's 1871 topographic and scientific survey stretching from northern Nevada to southern Arizona, the first official exploration of southern Nevada's interior. The expedition was divided into two groups, with Lyle in command of one. He explored an area from north of Belmont south and west to the San Antonio Mountains, Fish Lake Valley, Camp Independence, the Telescope Range, Death Valley, and Ash Meadows, crossing the Colorado River and eventually reaching Tucson, Arizona. At one point the route took them to Rose Spring in the Telescope Range, across Death Valley via Furnace Creek, to Ash Meadows. In his report, Lyle wrote,

Two days' hard marching brought our worn-out train to Ash Meadows, where we found plenty of excellent grass and water, the latter from Warm Springs. Very little wood here. To reach this point we had to cross the Funeral Mountains, a range quite high and steep, and the Amargosa Desert, through which, for miles, the dry bed of the river of that name meanders southward (Wheeler, 1871:84).

Several years later Lyle described Ash Meadows and the importance such springs held for the early desert travelers:

To those who have experienced the pangs of thirst, while journeying over the desolate wastes that characterize this section, it will not be surprising that reminiscences of water should linger longest in the memory of the traveler. In fact the procurement of that necessity is a matter of such vital importance that all movements are subordinated and controlled by the answer to the question, "Is there any water there?" Should the reply be in the negative, some other route must be followed, or else a supply of water must be carried along. The springs in this portion of the Great Basin are few, and often far between (Lyle, 1878:18).

Lyle described one spring in Ash Meadows (probably Fairbanks Spring):

Upon the eastern edge of the Amargoza Desert is quite a large area called Ash Meadows; so named from a small species of ash tree growing there. The meadows are covered with good grass and are well watered by numerous warm springs.

The principal spring was about thirty feet in diameter and situated at the foot of a small butte. The water issued from the bottom, through a tufaceous mass of rock.

It was about four or five feet deep and was cooler than

the other springs. The stream of water that flowed out was five inches deep and two feet wide, and clear as crystal. The sides and bottom of this spring were covered with a white, chalky-looking deposit, that gave a milky tinge to the water when stirred up. A few small fish were seen in this spring. Many of the springs in this vicinity contained quicksand (Lyle, 1878:24-25).

Squires (1955:334) wrote that in 1876 Joseph Yount and Charles W. Towner, accompanied by their families, were camped on the Amargosa Desert when Indians drove off their herd of horses. Shortly afterward, Towner purchased the Indian Springs and Yount purchased what was to become the Manse Ranch in Pahrump Valley. Doherty (1974:165) contended that the horses were not run off, but that many were killed by renegade Indians in the vicinity of what eventually became the Johnnie Mine, where Yount had left the animals to graze. By the late 1860s, small mining operations had started at the north end of Death Valley, and by the early 1870s small mining operations were in full swing in the Panamint Mountains, where William M. Stewart, Nevada's senior senator, was an active partner in both mining and various mining promotions (Lingenfelter, 1986:101, 117).

CHAPTER 3

Early Settlers

here were many attractive sites that were suitable for agriculture and ranching in the Amargosa region. One of the best was Ash Meadows. However, until the mining boom in the Death Valley area in the 1870s, these sites were too far from markets to encourage settlers. Prospectors and miners who arrived with the boom provided a market that made viable agricultural sites that were once of little economic value. Moreover, the availability of locally produced foodstuffs was an obvious advantage to the miners.

Cattle and Crops

The first white man to settle in the Amargosa Valley was Charles King. King was a Yankee who had gone to California with the Gold Rush in 1850. By 1870 he had worked as a lighterer on San Francisco Bay, a merchant in Sacramento, a lumberman at Yankee Jim, a sheriff in Placer County, and a miner all over California and Nevada. King was working as a miner in Timpahute in Lincoln County, Nevada, in the sum-

mer of 1871 when Wheeler's survey came through, and he
signed on as a guide. King turned out to be a very good guide
for Wheeler; other guides died in the heat of the summer of
1871. King used his position with Wheeler to examine business prospects in the areas through which he traveled. With
mining operations at Ivanpah and Chloride Cliff, and others
opening in the nearby hills, King recognized that rangeland in
Ash Meadows would be valuable. With its perennial springs
and seeps, Ash Meadows contained thousands of acres of virgin grasslands. All he need do was claim it (Lingenfelter,
1986:166).

With backing from Pioche mining superintendent Charles
Forman, King purchased a herd of 1300 head of cattle in
southern California and drove them to Ash Meadows in
January 1873, where the cattle had free range. King reasoned
he could purchase his cattle for a few cents a pound on the hoof
in California, fatten them up at his Ash Meadows ranch, and
sell them to miners in the vicinity for more than 30 cents a
pound, slaughtered. Though alkali, black leg, and Paiute
arrows took their toll on King's cattle, his operation was
successful. The next year he opened a butcher shop at
Panamint, across Death Valley. King's beef was worth more
per ton than the ore being mined in the Panamint Mountains,
some of which was being shipped all the way to England for
processing. In 1875 King sold his half of the partnership to
Gold Hill butcher L. T. Fox and moved on. He built a stone
house at what is now the Point of Rocks Spring in Ash
Meadows (Lingenfelter, 1986:166-167).

In the winter of 1874-1875, the Lee Brothers, Philander and
Leander (known as Phi and Cub), both in their early twenties,
staked out a spring near King. They brought with them a herd
of cattle from the San Joaquin Valley, and they took Paiute

wives. The Lee brothers were known for the tales they spun, and many tales were told about them (Lingenfelter, 1986:167).

In the fall of 1879, Eugene Lander started a ranch near the present town of Beatty. By the end of the 1870s, most of the springs and seeps along the Amargosa River from Beatty south and in the Pahrump Valley had been taken up by homesteaders (Lingenfelter, 1986:167). By the early 1880s, the decline of mines in the Ivanpah and Tecopa areas had deprived ranchers and farmers of markets, and about half had been forced to abandon their homesteads (Lingenfelter, 1986:168).

Most of the homesteads in the Amargosa area during this period were 160-acre claims. The homesteaders were generally unable to irrigate more than a fraction of the claim, however. During the mining booms, most of the homesteads were hay ranches, since alfalfa was a profitable crop providing the most return for work expended. Farmers could get four cuttings a year and the yield was about 6 tons to the acre. Hay was worth anywhere from $70 to $200 a ton in the mining camps, depending on the market. Farmers also raised barley, for which they could obtain $200 a ton, but the yield was only about 2 tons per acre. They also raised vegetables, including corn, beans, potatoes, beets, cabbages, onions, squash, and melons, for which they also could receive $200 a ton. For those who planted trees, such as apples, peaches, pears, figs, plums, apricots, nectarines, almonds, and walnuts, the payoff was over $500 a ton. A few ranchers raised grapes and made wine. Nearly all ranchers kept stock but, unlike King, none had more than 100 head (Lingenfelter, 1986:168-169). Houses ranged from brush and mud *jacals* to adobe and stone structures. Some had wooden floors with cellars and cool verandas (Lingenfelter, 1986:169).

Longstreet: Legendary Settler

Andrew Jackson (Jack) Longstreet was a southerner, but little is known of the first 40 years of his life. He may have been born in Louisiana in 1838; no one knows for sure (Zanjani, 1987; 1988). Even his name may not have been real, but one chosen from the gallery of southern heroes—Andrew Jackson, idol of the Battle of New Orleans, and General James Longstreet, hero of the southwestern Confederacy (Zanjani, 1988:153). One source (Lewis, 1969:3) stated that Jack Longstreet claimed General Longstreet was his brother. In any event, it was a high-profile name not necessarily selected for concealment, but "chosen by a man proud and defiant enough to fly his heroes like a banner over his second life with the certainty that none would dare to question him too closely" (Zanjani, 1988:153).

Longstreet was a quintessential frontiersman, as reflected in the title of Sally Zanjani's (1988) biography on this man of the West, *Jack Longstreet: Last of the Desert Frontiersmen*. Longstreet was said to have had five notches on his gun and was described as "the most perfect typification of the Old West's gunman" (Lingenfelter, 1986:168). He wore his hair long to cover his ears, which had been cropped for horse stealing when he was a youth (Zanjani, 1988:8–9).

Longstreet was first seen in the northern Arizona territory in the 1880s. And after having run a saloon in the Mormon communities on the Muddy River, he took up residence in Oasis Valley north of Beatty, where he and two other men were the only white residents in 7000 square miles (Zanjani, 1987). Longstreet ran a tent saloon at Sylvania in the Sylvania Mountains; there he prospected for the Breyfogle gold and became involved in a scrape for "administering 'Indian justice' to an unpopular mining superintendent" (Lingenfelter, 1986:168).

Several years later, Longstreet homesteaded in Ash Meadows, building a stone cabin near the spring which today bears his name; the remains of the cabin were destroyed by flood waters in the early 1980s. He knew the Death Valley country well and possessed many desert survival skills. While living in Ash Meadows, Longstreet was involved in a "claim-jumping shoot-out" at the Chespa Mine, located just to the east (Lingenfelter, 1986:168), and perhaps a protracted gunfight at his cabin, which he survived because his enemies could not smoke him out since he had access to the water flowing from a spring inside his cabin (Zanjani, 1988:76). Most of the details of Longstreet's life in Ash Meadows, however, are "lost in the sun-drenched silence that enshrouded the remote southern country" of Nevada (Zanjani, 1988:76).

Longstreet was long an advocate of Indian rights while in Nevada, spoke Paiute, and was married to an Ash Meadows Paiute woman, Fannie Black. In December 1899, Longstreet bought a ranch at Hawes Canyon located on the west side of the Kawich Mountains, east of Tonopah, where he and Fannie moved. He kept the ranch at Ash Meadows until 1906. About the same time he sold the Hawes Canyon ranch and homesteaded in the Monitor Range, where he also operated a mine. He resided there until his death in 1928. He is buried in the cemetery at Belmont, Nevada.

The great boom at Tonopah began in 1900, shortly after Longstreet moved to Hawes Canyon. Old-timers in Tonopah remember him as an old man: a strong, almost austere, figure. When Longstreet died, several curious people are said to have checked his ears to see if they were really cropped. Results of the checking are not known but it is believed that the story proved true.

An unverifiable story told in Tonopah suggests that even in death, the old gunfighter might have gotten the last word.

Longstreet's car, it seems, had been left at the Mizpah Garage in Tonopah. Lee Henderson, owner of the garage and one of those who had checked Longstreet for cropped ears, was going through Longstreet's belongings in the car when the deceased's six-shooter, hidden among the belongings, accidentally fell to the cement floor and discharged, wounding Henderson in the leg (Slavin, 1989).

CHAPTER 4

Life in the Amargosa Valley in the 1880s

lthough settlers had resided in the Amargosa for more than ten years by the middle of the 1880s, we have very few descriptions from this period. No doubt the isolation, spartan existence, and the rarity of visitors account for the dearth of writings. None but the most motivated of travelers would have kept a record of events, places, and people. Two accounts have survived.

A Buckboard Journey Across the Amargosa

In 1886 T. W. Brooks traveled from southern California to Oasis Valley by buckboard, and he recorded his experiences and observations. He spent several days with the Younts at their ranch in Pahrump Valley and described Ash Meadows:

> On the 11th of March with fresh supplies, we left the Yount Ranch, drove 32 miles, and camped at the Stone House, formerly owned by Mr. Lee. At this camp there is plenty of wood and water. It is at one of the many very large warm springs which burst forth from the side of the moun-

tain amidst a lime formation. The water being warm it dissolves more or less of the combination of mineral in the locality and, as the water becomes partially congealed, it deposits a substance resembling a cream-colored lining along the course of the stream, forming beautiful little banks upon either side; and in this locality the accumulation has closed over, forming a meandering and strange looking trough, through which the water goes rumbling down the hill. This has been a great resort for the Paiute Indians. Many relics and grinding stones are to be seen, which from the great wear of the hole in the rock we suppose they have been used for hundreds of years.

On the morning of the 12th we left the Stone House and traveling in a northerly direction a distance of 20 miles arrived at Mr. Scott's ranch and camped for the day. The interest at this place is another large warm water spring similar to the last described, but inasmuch as we are now in a part of the noted Ash Meadows it will not be amiss to allude to the peculiarities of this section. Ash Meadows is a part of the middle or center of the great valley of the Amargosa river and lies southeast of the great level plains or valley. Its peculiarities and description to the eye is the great variety of minerals that are here concentrated and combined; salt, borax, soda, gypsum salt, sulphur, lime, etc., are here visible. The description of Ash Meadows proper is the interesting appearance of the vast extent of meadow grass. A view from some prominency of the great field of grass and the strip and clusters of ash timber affording shade, and the many springs of good water, and one contemplating a fine stock ranch, his heart might be gladened and he heard to exclaim, "I have found it."

"It is not all gold that glitters." I am told upon good authority that the minerals that exist in this locality have the affect of relaxing or weakening the cattle in the joints, and especially in the knee joint, and that from inability to stand upon their feet they are obliged to gather their food and travel upon their knees; also, that the hoofs of the cattle grow to enormous length of twelve to fourteen inches.

Mr. Scott's station is of importance to the country beyond, and this is the last water before crossing the lava plains of forty miles.

Leaving the Scott ranch or station on the 13th, we were well supplied with water, traveled north a distance of 30 miles, and made a dry camp at Volcano Wash. In the midst of a level plain, forty-five by thirty miles, looking northeast, a beautiful cone-shaped mountain can be seen. The composition of its surface is such as produces a bright, life-like appearance of variegated colors. In its top, though not discernible in the distance, is a center depression or cavity in the shape of a flanged funnel with its receiving end up; this, however, is not perfect, as one side or part of the funnel-shaped hole has a narrow, deep cut which has served as a passage or outlet through which the lava has flown to many parts of this great plain. It is an extinct volcano. The neighboring hills and mountains are yet black from the fumes of the volcano (Brooks, 1970:13-17).

Accounts such as this are of great interest to both historians and residents of the area. In his notes to Brooks' manuscript, Anthony L. Lehman interpreted the route that Brooks must have taken from Pahrump across the Amargosa Valley. Lehman believes that on March 11, after leaving Yount's ranch, it seems likely that Brooks and his companions "moved on in a northwesterly direction, going either by way of Sixmile Spring (the most direct route) or perhaps detouring through the more level Stewart Valley farther to the west. The thirty-two miles covered would place their camp in the vicinity of several springs: Winters' Hole, Bole's Spring, or Big Spring. Winters' Hole seems to be the most likely spot, inasmuch as Aaron Winters is known to have lived in a stone house there and, furthermore, the spring at this site emanated from the side of a rock hill" (Brooks, 1970:40).

Lehman also suggests that Mr. Scotts' ranch, at which Brooks arrived on March 12, is probably what later became Fairbanks Spring Ranch at Fairbanks Spring (Brooks, 1970: 40). Lehman's contention has been closely examined by long-time Amargosa area resident and historian Deke Lowe (1989). Lowe, who knows the area as well as — perhaps better than— anyone else, has pointed out that Lehman's interpretation of Brooks' route after leaving the Manse Ranch in Pahrump Valley doesn't "add up." Brooks reports traveling 20 miles the twelfth day; yet Lehman only has him going from Winters' Hole to Fairbanks Spring, which are only 2 or 3 miles apart. Lowe believes that information from the original text may have accidentally been dropped or transposed; or it is possible that another route would better explain Brooks' description.

The "dry camp at Volcano Wash" where Brooks camped on the night of the thirteenth, Lehman believes, is "the mouth of Crater Flat where it debouches into the Amargosa Desert" (Brooks, 1970:41).

The Frontier Home of Aaron and Rosie Winters

Aaron and Rosie Winters were among the best-known early residents of the Amargosa Valley (Warren, 1980:225). They lived in a stone house at Ash Meadows in "abject poverty" at the time of the following description (Lee, 1930:132). It is said Winters had killed two men and was thus "a highly respected member of the most exclusive social circle of the desert" (Spears, 1892:56). The Winters apparently were in the area by the end of the 1870s (Lingenfelter, 1986:167). The house they lived in probably originally belonged to Charles King and Grant [Charles] Forman, whose names appear on the map for the water rights filing in Lincoln County in 1871 (Warren, 1980:225). The following account of the Winters' home, which is said to have been a typical residence of the area, was written by C. M. Plumb, who visited the Winters. It appeared in John R. Spears' classic volume, *Illustrated Sketches of Death Valley.*

Close against the hill, one side half-hewn out of the rock, stood a low stone building, with a tule-thatched roof. The single room within was about fifteen feet square. In front was a canvas-covered addition of about the same size. The earth, somewhat cleared of broken rock originally there, served as a floor for both rooms. There was a door to the stone structure, and directly opposite this was a fire-place, while a cook-stove stood on a projecting rock at one side of it. At the right was a bed, and at the foot of the bed a few shelves for dishes. A cotton curtain was stretched over some clothing hanging on wooden pegs in the corner.

On the other side was the lady's boudoir—a curiosity in its way. There was a window with a deep ledge there. A newspaper with a towel covered the ledge, in the center of which was a starch box supporting a small looking-glass. On each side of the mirror hung old brushes, badly worn bits of ribbon and some other fixings for the hair. Handy by was a lamp-mat, lying on another box, and covered with bottles of Hogan's Magnolia Balm, Felton's Gossamer for the Complexion, and Florida Water—all, alas, empty, but still cherished by the wife, a comely, delicate Spanish-American woman with frail health and little fitted for the privations of the desert.

The shelves about the room and the rude mantle over
the fire-place were spread with covers made of notched
sheets of newspaper. Two rocking chairs had little tidies on
their backs. The low flat pillows were covered with pillow
shams and the bed itself with a tawny spread. In place of a
library there were a number of copies of the *Police Gazette*.
There was a flour barrel against the wall, a small bag of rice
near by, and two or three sacks of horse feed in a corner. The
sugar, coffee, and tea were kept under the bed.

The water of the spring ran down the hill and formed a
pool in front of the house, and here a number of ducks and
chickens, with a pig and big dog, formed a happy group, a
group that rambled about in the house as well as romped
beside the water of the spring. A few cattle grazed on the
bunch-grass of the valley that stretched away before the
house, gray and desolate (Spears, 1892:56-57).

The Discovery of Borax in Death Valley

The poverty experienced by Aaron and Rosie Winters was
soon relieved by a stroke of luck. Borax was discovered in
Death Valley in 1873, but even at $700 a ton the remote location
made the deposits unprofitable; more accessible deposits to
the west were worked instead (Lingenfelter, 1986:173). In
1881, news of the possible extension of the Carson and Colorado Railroad south through Owens Valley and the Southern
Pacific east across the Mojave had stimulated interest in borax
in the surrounding area. This news caused a handful of
prospectors to seek out the mineral. One such prospector was
Henry Spiller, who chanced to spend the night at Winters'
ranch in Ash Meadows. He told Winters about borax deposits
in Nevada and the fortune awaiting the man who could find
more borax. After sunset Spiller took out a sample of borax
and showed Winters how to test for it by pouring alcohol and

sulphuric acid on the salt. Winters watched with attention, for he had remembered seeing a mineral in Death Valley that resembled what Spiller had shown him (Spears, 1892:58).

When Spiller left, Aaron and Rosie Winters went to the valley. They gathered likely looking samples, and that night tested them as Spiller had instructed. "At last, when the shadows had closed in around them, Winters put some of the salt into a saucer, poured the acid and alcohol on them, and with trembling hands struck a match. It was an anxious moment. Then he shouted, 'She burns green, Rosie! We're rich, by God!'" (Lingenfelter, 1986:174). Winters staked out his claims, and he eventually sold them for $20,000 to San Francisco borax magnate William T. Coleman, who at that time had a virtual monopoly on American borax; the claim was developed into the Harmony Borax Works (Lingenfelter, 1986:174; Warren, 1980:221). Winters used the money to purchase the "even better-developed Pahrump Ranch" from Charles Bennett in May 1882 (Lingenfelter, 1986:174; Warren, 1980:225-226). Rosie died a short time later and Winters lost all but a small part of the ranch for taxes in 1887 (Lingenfelter, 1986:175).

The Lee brothers, Phi and Cub, the Winters' former neighbors in Ash Meadows, went on to discover borax deposits that dwarfed those Winters had found. The Lila C., located by Phi and Cub, produced millions of dollars in borax, and the Monte Blanco deposit, found by Phi and two partners, still holds several million tons of borax ore. Phi Lee and his partners sold their Monte Blanco claims for $4000. Phi used his share to buy a ranch at Resting Spring, where he resided until 1915. At that point he traded the Resting Spring Ranch for one in the Charleston Mountains that had a large, flowing spring. He lived there until the early 1920s. He died in Riverside, California, a few years later (Lingenfelter, 1986:175; D. Lowe, 1989).

CHAPTER 5

The Railroads Come to the Amargosa Valley

I n the early 1900s the Amargosa Valley had few resources that were of interest to the outside world. Thus, its fate was tied to economic developments that occurred elsewhere. In reality, the exploitation of mineral deposits in Death Valley, the discovery of silver and gold in the Tonopah-Goldfield area, the founding of Las Vegas in 1905, and the short-lived Bullfrog mining district boom all were important in the next phase of the history of the Amargosa Valley.

Clark Builds the LV&T

By January 1905, Senator William A. Clark had completed his San Pedro, Los Angeles and Salt Lake Railroad (the SP, LA&SL), linking Los Angeles and Salt Lake City (Myrick, 1963:455). In just a few months the railroad would hold land auctions, which would mark the real beginnings of the city of Las Vegas. In 1872 F. M. (Borax) Smith had discovered borax ore at Teel's Marsh, northwest of Bellville, Nevada. In 1890 he acquired William T. Coleman's borax holdings in Death Valley and Borate (Calico), California (Lingenfelter, 1986:185). In that same year Smith formed the Pacific Coast Borax Company. After 1900 the Calico ore began to run low, and Smith found it necessary to turn to the Lila C., named after his daughter and located in the Funeral Mountains on the eastern edge of Death Valley. He needed a railroad to remove the ore from the remote area, so Smith incorporated his Tonopah and Tidewater Railroad (the T&T) in New Jersey in July 1904 (Myrick, 1963:455, 545-546). Smith had conducted surveys to determine the best route to follow in order to reach the Lila C. One such route began in Las Vegas, where it would connect with Senator Clark's SP, LA&SL Railroad. Smith felt that Clark was in favor of such a connection and began making plans for the line's construction (Myrick, 1963:545-546).

Meanwhile, major discoveries of precious metals were made in several districts in southern Nevada, most notably at Bullfrog in the mountains at the head of the Amargosa Valley. Tonopah and Goldfield were developing rapidly. Clark began having second thoughts concerning Borax Smith's plans (Myrick, 1963:546). He decided to survey his own route from Las Vegas to Tonopah, and on September 22, 1905, Clark incorporated the Las Vegas and Tonopah Railroad (Myrick, 1963:461). Smith, believing that Clark was in agreement with his plans, unfortunately started constructing his roadbed north out of Las Vegas. In August 1905, Clark denied Smith rights to connect to the SP, LA&SL, and Smith was forced to abandon his Las Vegas connection. In October, Clark took over Smith's operations in Las Vegas, including the terminal and the grading that Smith had completed. Clark's railroad headed north out of Las Vegas with stops at Tule Springs, Corn Creek, Owens, Indian Springs, Charleston, through the Point of Rocks gap west of Mercury, and out into the Amargosa Valley, with stops at Johnnie Siding and at Amargosa (both at the base of the Specter Range) and at Rose's Well northeast of Big Dune, and on into Beatty and Rhyolite (Myrick, 1963:464-465, 471). On Friday, October 12, 1906, the first regular passenger service from Las Vegas to Gold Center, located at the Beatty Narrows, arrived; six days later the last two miles of track to Beatty were placed in regular operation (Myrick 1963:475). When completed, the railroad went to Rhyolite and all the way to Goldfield (Myrick, 1963:489).

The Las Vegas and Tonopah Railroad (LV&T) operated until October 31, 1918, when, despite local protests, it ceased operation due to declines in passengers and operating revenues (Myrick, 1963:502). The rails were removed and the equipment and rolling stock were dispersed; the locomotives operated on the San Diego and Arizona Eastern and on the Northwestern Pacific for some years (Myrick, 1963:502-503). In 1919, the Nevada Department of Highways purchased claims to the Las Vegas and Tonopah roadbed for $3889.44 and incorporated it into the state highway system (Myrick, 1963:503).

Smith Builds the T&T

Following his troubles with Senator Clark, Borax Smith turned his attentions to another route. He shifted the T&T's base of operations from Las Vegas to Ludlow, California. He had been assured by the Santa Fe Railroad that it would cooperate with his efforts to build a railroad to his Lila C. Mine and northward to the boomtowns of Rhyolite, Goldfield, and Tonopah. Though the Las Vegas route would have been shorter, Borax Smith had no choice in the matter. The grading equipment was moved overland from Las Vegas to Ludlow, passing through the Pahrump Valley. The route to Gold Center from Ludlow was 167 miles; by comparison it was 118 miles if Las Vegas was used as the starting point (Myrick, 1963:547).

On November 19, 1905, the first T&T rails were laid at Ludlow (Myrick, 1963:547). Going north from Ludlow, the T&T crossed the Union Pacific's tracks at Crucero, then passed Soda Lake, Razor, and continued on to Silver Lake (Myrick, 1963:548). "The first 75 miles of track, to a point just beyond Dumont, were completed by May 1906" (Myrick, 1963:548). Over the next 12 miles to Tecopa the track descended from a plateau into the Amargosa River canyon and traversed its length along the side walls of the gorge. This involved construction of large cuts and long fills, including "three major trestles of up to 500 feet in length" (Myrick, 1963:548). The heat in the canyon in the summer of 1906 made the retention of workers difficult and thereby increased expenses. It took approximately one year for Smith to complete the 12-mile canyon section (Myrick, 1963:555). By the middle of October 1907, there was regular service on the 144 miles of rail between Ludlow and Leeland in the Amargosa Valley. On October 30, 1907, the last spike was driven at Gold Center. Smith's Tonopah and Tidewater Railroad had reached Gold Center over a year after Senator Clark's Las Vegas and Tonopah line (Myrick, 1963:556). The 12 miles of construction in the Amargosa Canyon, signs of a slowing boom in Rhyolite, and concerns about Goldfield and Tonopah all were discouraging, and the T&T officials decided against building any track north of Gold Center. Instead, arrangements were made to connect with John Brock's Bullfrog Goldfield Railroad and to use its track from Gold Center northward to Beatty and westward to Bullfrog and Rhyolite (Myrick, 1963:556).

In early December 1907, Pullman passenger service was inaugurated between the Beatty area and Los Angeles over the T&T and Santa Fe tracks, which was a shorter route to southern California than the LV&T via Clark's lines connecting in Las Vegas. The price of a ticket from Beatty to Los Angeles was $16.25, and a round trip fare cost $26.00 (Myrick, 1963:556). Spur lines on the T&T Railroad were constructed at Tecopa, Death Valley Junction, the Lila C. Mine, and Ash Meadows (Myrick, 1963:548). In 1914, the T&T's arrangement for use of the Bullfrog Goldfield Railroad's tracks to the north of Goldfield was terminated, with the T&T maintaining trackage rights only from Gold Center to Beatty (Myrick, 1963:586). The LV&T was combined with the Bullfrog Goldfield Railroad from Beatty, although the latter line retained its name. With the closure of the LV&T in 1918, the T&T took over the Bullfrog Goldfield route north to Goldfield (Myrick, 1963:586).

During the peak of marble quarry operations at Carrara in 1915 and 1916, the LV&T Railroad served the town. Quarrying operations folded prior to the demise of that railroad. When the quarry reopened in the late 1920s, the T&T was the only railroad left in the area, and a 3/4-mile spur was built across the valley from the T&T tracks to the siding at Carrara in 1927. The branch was torn up in 1932 (Myrick, 1963:587-588).

The last train traveled on the Bullfrog Goldfield Railroad tracks in January 1928. During the late 1920s Pullman service from Los Angeles to Beatty was available three times weekly via the Santa Fe; by 1930 the service was down to only one train a week. By 1933, the T&T's feud with the SP, LA & SL was long since past, the 26-mile section between Ludlow (on the Santa Fe) and Crucero (on the Salt Lake route) had been closed, and the T&T's shops were moved from Ludlow to Death Valley Junction. By 1939, the T&T equipment consisted of only 4 locomotives, 1 motor car, 29 freight cars, and 4 passenger cars. Between 1933 and 1938 revenues never exceeded $124,000 a year and were as low as $76,000; in 1920, by comparison, the revenues had been $600,000. In 1939 a mixed train of freight and passengers ran twice a week all the way from Crucero to Beatty (Myrick, 1963:591). On June 14, 1940, all operations ceased (Myrick, 1963:593). By the summer of 1943, all rails on the T&T had been removed and its equipment dispersed. Many bridge timbers and ties from the historic railroad were used in the construction of buildings in the Mojave Desert area (Myrick, 1963:593).

The T&T was more than just a railroad to the people occupying the desert stretching from Ludlow, California, to Tonopah, Nevada. It was an institution, a prominent economic and social fixture in their lives. As Myrick (1963:588) said,

> Operating as it did over some 250 miles of desert country railroad, the T&T became a lifeline for the scattered people living in the area. Over the course of the decades, the railroad men and the townspeople came to know each other well, no doubt far better than those along larger railroads of similar circumstances. In talking with people today—whether they be former employees, former patrons, or merely neighbors—thoughts of the T&T bring back many friendly recollections.

The railroad's end left a gap in the scattered desert communities it served, which, like the passing of an old friend, has never been filled.

CHAPTER 6

People and Places —
The Early 1900s

y the early 1900s, the population of the Amargosa region had begun to grow. Growth brought an increase in opportunity for enterprising people. Freight was being moved north to Tonopah and to camps in the Death Valley area. Virtually every water hole was occupied. The proliferation of camps provided a succession of opportunities for miners, merchants, and desperadoes. In the Amargosa, formerly worthless deposits of clay soon became valuable.

"Dad" Fairbanks

Ralph Jacobus "Dad" Fairbanks is one of the best-known individuals in the history of the Amargosa-Death Valley region. The Fairbanks family originally came from Massachusetts. Dad Fairbanks' mother, Susan Manderville, was descended from early Dutch families who colonized Manhattan Island shortly after its exploration by Henry Hudson (Lisle, 1974a:4). The old Fairbanks family home, which still stands in Dedham, Massachusetts, was built in 1636 and is now a state historical park. Prior to being taken over by the government, the home's ownership never passed out of the Fairbanks family. David and Susan Fairbanks, the parents of Dad Fairbanks, were people of means in the mercantile business in Massachusetts. Upon being converted by Mormon missionaries, they sold everything and moved to Utah, arriving about 1846 (C. Lowe, 1988).

Dad Fairbanks was born in 1857 in Payson, Utah, the tenth child in the family. He received a taste of pioneering early in life when, in 1865, his family was called by the church to settle in St. Joseph on the Muddy River in Nevada (Lisle, 1974a:4). While a resident of St. Joseph, he made several trips with his father to the Gass Ranch in the Las Vegas Valley, once in the company of Mormon missionary Jacob Hamblin. On one such trip he played with the son of Paiute Indian Chief Tecopa in the Las Vegas Creek; he is known to have spoken at least one Indian language. He once made a trip from Bonnelli's Landing on the Colorado River to Fort Mojave, camping along the way at Callville, El Dorado Canyon, and Cottonwood Island (Lisle, 1974a:4).

When Fairbanks was ten, his family returned to their farm in Payson. As he matured (he grew to a height of 6'2"), he worked at a variety of jobs; he was employed for a number of years at the Payson Mercantile Store, which he later remarked provided him with the best education of his life. When he was 18 years old he and one of his brothers signed on as swampers on a wagon train bound for San Bernardino. The trip west of Las Vegas was the beginning of an intimate association with that desert region. On the return trip from San Bernardino, Dad and his brother looked for work in the mines around Pioche. Although he found little work, Dad learned about prospecting and soon developed a reputation as a first-rate poker player. When he returned to Payson the next spring after having "jack-assed around over most of Nevada from Idaho to the Colorado River," he had a sizable bankroll (Lisle, 1974a:5). Once home, Dad found the rural, agrarian life in the Payson area uninteresting.

In 1883 Dad and an older brother were called by the Mormon Church to help establish a new colony on the Sevier River in southern Utah. There he filed on a homestead near the newly created community of Annabella, not far from Richfield, Utah. In the meantime, Dad had married his childhood sweetheart, Celestia, and the couple and their young children moved into a two-room cabin Dad had built on the homestead. He acquired the name "Dad" because Indians often heard Celestia and the children address him as "Dad" and assumed that was his name (Lisle, 1974a:5). Not really a farmer, Dad was responsible for running the colony's small freighting operation from the nearby mountains. He hauled logs for firewood and for constructing houses, farm buildings, and fences (Lisle, 1974a:5).

Though the Fairbanks family had a good home and plenty to eat, Dad was not satisfied with opportunities for money-making in the community. He constantly strove for a more prosperous life. In addition, he found himself in dispute with the local townspeople. His homestead was located on beautiful pasture on the edge of the Sevier River, and many local residents pastured their cattle and horses there. After a few years, he asked them to remove their stock from his property and threatened to confiscate the animals if they did not act quickly. The townspeople did not remove the livestock; true to his word, Dad sold the stock, outraging his neighbors and many other community members. The community of Annabella, and Dad's participation in the colonization of the town, had been organized under the auspices of the United Order, a Mormon organization that practiced the concept of shared labor and shared participation in the products of labor. As a result of his confiscatory acts, Dad was excommunicated from the Mormon Church (C. Lowe, 1988).

By 1902, Senator Clark was in the process of constructing his SP, LA & SL Railroad, which would connect Salt Lake and Los Angeles. Dad, who was an expert teamster and always interested in new enterprise, obtained a contract for grading on the new railroad's roadbed. His contract called for road work between Caliente and Las Vegas. Upon completion of Clark's railroad, Dad Fairbanks found himself in Las Vegas. In the spring of 1905 Borax Smith began construction on his proposed T&T Railroad, which would link Las Vegas with Tonopah. When Borax Smith encountered problems with Senator Clark and moved his railroad operations to Ludlow, California, Dad continued to work on Clark's LV&T Railroad. He obtained contracts for hauling and for grading sections of the roadbed between Las Vegas and Beatty. When the LV&T reached Beatty, Dad obtained similar contracts on the T&T. He also hauled ore from the mines in the area to the nearest railheads as well as supplies in and out of Rhyolite. In these activities he was assisted by his sons, who were all skilled teamsters (C. Lowe, 1988).

During this period Dad purchased the Ash Meadows spring and nearby land, which now bears the Fairbanks name, from "Kit" Carson (not the original Kit Carson) for $2000. At his Fairbanks Spring Ranch, Dad established a mercantile business known as Fairbanks Mercantile and a freighting business between the railhead at Johnnie and the booming community of Greenwater, located south of Ash Meadows on the brink of Death Valley. Fairbanks is said to have hauled the first load of freight into Greenwater in the summer of 1905 (Belden, 1954:34). He also established freighting businesses in and out of area boomtowns, which had sprung up under the stimulus of the discoveries at Rhyolite (C. Lowe, 1988).

Fairbanks Spring afforded an unusually good supply of water, and travelers through the Amargosa Valley often camped there. At his mercantile store, which functioned as a trading post, Dad Fairbanks sold various mining supplies, including picks, shovels, dynamite—anything a miner might need. He also sold hay, grain, and feed. The ample pasture in the area also offered grazing for Dad's stock as well as the animals of travelers. Dad also grubstaked substantial numbers of prospectors, an enterprise in which he engaged until his last years. In addition to his other activities, he also ran a boardinghouse. The Kimball Brothers ran a daily stage over the 50 miles from Johnnie Siding on the LV&T Railroad to Greenwater. The fare was $18, took two days, and the passengers and drivers spent the night at Fairbanks' Ranch (Lingenfelter, 1986:322).

Once he had established himself at Fairbanks Spring, Dad sent for his wife and daughters, who were still in Annabella. The family in Annabella was very excited about the move to Ash Meadows, although Celesta, the Fairbanks' eldest daughter (named for her mother), regretted leaving. She was in love with a young man from Annabella, but Dad would not allow his daughters to marry until they were 18. The family traveled from Annabella to Cove Fort, Utah, by wagon; there they boarded the train to Las Vegas, where they spent the night in the Overland Hotel. The Overland was one of the first hotels in Las Vegas and was little more than a very large tent, with the rooms being partitioned only by canvas. The next day the family boarded the LV&T for the ride to Johnnie Siding, where Dad was to meet them. They rode on an open-air flatcar, with Mrs. Fairbanks becoming more and more depressed by the bleakness of the area in contrast to the more verdant Annabella. Celestia and her daughters were met at Johnnie Siding by her son David. Her impression was that the spot must have been the bleakest on the face of the earth, with nothing but desert as far as the eye could see. But she never complained (C. Lowe, 1988).

The conditions at Fairbanks Spring were better. There were some trees and plenty of grass and water. Dad had already set up a tent for Celestia and the girls and they found business was good, with plenty of work for everyone. In fact, with the extra help, business further prospered. Hay was sold by the ton and gasoline was stocked in 5-gallon tin cans. In addition to the store and a barn (both tents), there was a tent that served as a restaurant and 1905 version of a motel, a row of tents where travelers could stop and sleep overnight. Celestia served as the cook for the restaurant and the boardinghouse, a job she kept regardless of where the family moved.

At Fairbanks Spring, the younger Celesta Fairbanks found a new love. John Q. (Jack) Lisle had come from his home in California to Greenwater, where he had located a claim and was working it. One day Lisle started down to Fairbanks Spring with his burros and was camped in a dry wash for the night. A flash flood struck in the dark and washed away his bedroll and clothes and drove off his burros. He barely escaped with his life, and he was forced to walk to Fairbanks Spring a few miles away clad only in his long red beard and underwear. It was in such attire that he met his wife-to-be, Celesta. Lisle continued working his Greenwater claims for another two years, then sold out for $80,000, as family members recall. After Jack and Celesta were married, they moved to California; they also lived in Ely and Fernley, Nevada. Some years later they returned to Ash Meadows with their children (C. Lowe, 1988).

The famous sometimes passed through Fairbanks Spring.

One renowned traveler was Diamond-tooth Lil with her troupe. Diamond Lil was a flamboyant, wild-living woman who had a 1/3-carat diamond centered in a gold cap on one of her front teeth to attract attention to herself. Diamond Lil had been in Goldfield when she and several of her girls left the LV&T at the Johnnie Siding on the way to Greenwater, where she was to control the "red light" district for a short time (Brennan, 1975:30-31). They stayed overnight at Fairbanks Spring, as many travelers did. The young Fairbanks girls were enthralled with Diamond Lil and her girls and admired the beautiful dresses, with their bright colors in taffetas and satins. The best dress that the younger Celesta Fairbanks owned was gingham. Diamond-tooth Lil's arrival was an exciting event for the girls, but Dad would not let his daughters into the dining room or near Diamond Lil and her troupe because of their bad reputation. Diamondfield Jack, one of Diamond Lil's boyfriends, also visited Fairbanks Spring during this period (C. Lowe, 1988).

In 1908, Dad Fairbanks hitched up the wagons and moved Fairbanks Mercantile to Greenwater. He furnished essentially the same services in that boomtown as he had at Fairbanks Spring. The main reason for the relocation was the completion of the T&T and the reduced need for his freighting services in Ash Meadows. Dad Fairbanks stayed in Greenwater until 1910, and then he moved his mercantile business to Shoshone, which up to that time had been little more than an Indian camp. Once relocated in Shoshone, he hauled in deserted buildings from Greenwater and used them for houses, a store, and a restaurant (Belden, 1954:34). About this time the Fairbanks' daughter Stella married Charles A. Brown, who later became Dad's partner in Shoshone. Brown went on to serve as a California state senator from Inyo and Mono counties (C. Lowe, 1988).

In 1916, at the age of 60, Dad finally made his long hoped-for mining strike after he had been, as he said,

> jack-assing for thirty-five years trying to locate [it]. Strange as it may seem it wasn't gold I found, nor did I have to go very far to find it. I was browsing around out back of Shoshone one day and went into the Indian camp. There I found an Indian woman, Panamint Tom's squaw, washing her hair. She was doing it in an old gold pan full of something that looked like a mixture of mud and water and about the thickness of buttermilk. I watched her, and when she'd finished the job her hair was soft and clean and glossy. I asked where she got the stuff and she pointed out a certain hill. I immediately went to the hill, found a veritable mountain of valuable filtering clay, and staked out my claim on it.
>
> When I first started prospecting, this claim wouldn't have been worth a thin dime. But the change from oats to gasoline had made a big difference. I knew that this clay was extensively used in the refinement of petroleum and that, up to the time of my finding the deposit, the entire supply in this country had been imported (Lisle, 1974b:4-5).

Dad sold out to the Associated Oil Company in 1920. He is quoted as saying, "not being poverty-stricken, as the majority of prospectors usually are, I didn't have to select the first figure offered. So I hung onto it and shopped around for a buyer" (Lingenfelter, 1986:409). He wouldn't say how much he sold it for, only that it was a "tidy fortune—a comfortable stake for Dad Fairbanks and Mother for the rest of their days" (Lingenfelter, 1986:409).

In 1923 Dad Fairbanks bought 160 acres at the present site of Baker, California (Belden, 1954:34). In 1928, when he was past 70, he established a mercantile business there. In Baker, as always, the Fairbanks operation was a family business, a family concern. By this time, he and Celestia had 36 grandchildren, many of whom worked in the business at Baker, which included a gas station, a mercantile company, and a motel. One grandchild, Celesta Lisle Lowe, remembers him as "very stern." She recalled,

> He was all business. I felt like he was always too preoccupied to pay any attention to the little things that people did. He was a business man—he was worrying about business and making money and keeping the thing afloat. But if you ever needed anything, like you needed some money or you needed help, that was who you went to (C. Lowe, 1988).

Celestia, Dad's wife, was described by the same grandchild as,

> very gentle, a very devoted type person. On the surface, and to strangers seeing her, [you would] think she was a very meek little lady, but she really was not. She had a very tough character and she endured many things that weaker people would have broken under. She was faithful to her husband. She loved him very much. "Oh the dust. It's such dust" [she used to say in reference to their desert home]. She was, of course, born a Mormon, and she grew up that way and never forgot it (C. Lowe, 1988).

Dad and Celestia Fairbanks spent their last years in Santa Paula, California. Celestia died quietly in her sleep after 64 years of marriage. Their daughter Vonola said Dad came out of their bedroom one morning with a stricken look on his face. "Dad, what's wrong?" she asked.

"Poochie, I got to tell you something," he answered. "I called Mama when I woke up this morning but she didn't answer. When I looked over at her she was deader than hell!"

Dad Fairbanks, a pioneer of the desert, spent his last days

in a convalescent home in Hollywood, California. There he wondered, "why in the hell I don't die." He passed away October 4, 1943, at the age of 86 (Lisle, 1974b:5).

Outlaw Country

Old-timers from the Ash Meadows area reported that the vicinity was outlaw territory from the time of the first white settlers; a number of desperadoes often resided there. It is said that the Nye County sheriff was afraid to go to Ash Meadows; he saw little to gain by risking his life. The area's reputation lasted until the early 1930s (Revert, 1988; Toles, 1987), and people from there did not talk much about their past. Fred Davies, who lived in the area for many years before moving to Beatty, once found a skeleton in Ash Meadows with the bones of the hand still resting on an old blunderbuss. The weapon is said to be in a Carson City museum. No one knows who owned the gun (Reidhead, 1987). Such a place beyond the pale of the law probably had something to do with Jack Longstreet making his home there.

During the Prohibition Era of the 1920s and early 1930s, bootlegging was an important enterprise in the region. In 1931 there were at least six whiskey stills in Ash Meadows. The product was sold primarily in Las Vegas, but also to residents in Beatty, Death Valley Junction, Furnace Creek, and Shoshone. Fred Davies ran a still in Ash Meadows, and one of his best customers is reported to have been the governor of California. Davies was also known to poach on occasional unbranded cattle grazing in the Meadows; he would use them to feed the local Indians. The Indians in turn protected Davies' still and ran interference for him when enforcement agents lurked in the area (Reidhead, 1987). The isolated nature of life in Ash Meadows created ideal conditions for concealment of such activities. One long-time resident reported that bootleggers used to store their booze at a place called Bloody Gulch, located on the edge of Ash Meadows (Rooker, 1987).

The making of moonshine in Ash Meadows sometimes resulted in violence and bloodshed. On at least one occasion, children living in the Ash Meadows clay camp were witnesses to the grisly aftereffects of murder. In the mid-1920s, burros abandoned by prospectors roamed in and around the clay camp. A favorite pastime of the children was to put out feed to attract the burros, then catch, and ride them. The children and burros often headed for the refreshing waters of Crystal Springs, where the youngsters would swim before returning home (Lisle, 1989).

Ralph Lisle remembers a man in his fifties who lived in a cabin some 200 yards off the road that linked the clay camp and Crystal Springs. The man had concealed a still in some mesquites about 200 yards from his cabin. The children sometimes delivered messages and ran errands for the man, who seemed friendly and generous and often gave them peppermint-flavored hard candies (Lisle, 1989).

One day the children and burros, on their way to Crystal Springs, stopped by the house, expecting candy. They knocked on the door; no answer. They knocked again; only silence. Sensing something wrong, they looked in a window near the front door and could see nothing unusual. They then walked around to the back of the cabin and peeked into the window of the bedroom. They were horrified at what they saw. There on the bed beside the window lay their friend, dead. His entire chest was torn open by the blast from a shotgun fired at short range. Somebody had stuck the gun in the window and killed him while he slept. The terror at what the children saw was magnified by the fear that the murderer might try to kill them. Quickly they climbed on their burros and rode fast for home. Once home they told Ralph's father, John Quincy Lisle, what they had seen. In 1989 Ralph Lisle stated that he did not recall that the murder was ever solved (Lisle, 1989).

From the early 1920s until about 1925 or 1926, Wes Moreland operated a large saloon and brothel in the vicinity of Crystal Springs. He had previously owned a saloon in Las Vegas known as the Barrel House, and after leaving Ash Meadows he took over the depot in Rhyolite (Toles, 1987).

The Ash Meadows Clay Camps

The clay deposits in Ash Meadows are said to have been staked out and claimed about 1890 (Toles, 1987), but there was then no market for the clay. Word of Dad Fairbanks' 1916 discovery spread quickly, and many others came to the area to stake claims. A mining engineer named S. Frank Brock moved to the area and discovered an immense deposit of clay; he staked claim to over 6 square miles. It took him several years to convince oil companies that the clays, primarily hydrous magnesium silicates, were useful in cleaning or clarifying heavy oils. In 1918, Brock shipped several hundred tons of clay to Standard Oil for tests and more to other companies during the next few years. The southern California oil boom was in full swing, and by 1925 he had convinced at least five companies, including Associated, Pacific, Pan-American, Standard, Union Oil, and Standard's subsidiary, General Petroleum, to each buy a quarter section or more for a grand total of $350,000 (Lingenfelter, 1986:409-410).

General Petroleum, through its subsidiary, General Clay, began work in the area in 1925; by summer several companies were involved, with 50 men working, producing 1200 tons a month. Clay was removed from the pit, placed on a platform made of railroad ties and allowed to dry, then trucked to the Bradford Siding, 3 or 4 miles away, where it was loaded on the T&T Railroad (Lingenfelter, 1986:410). George Ishmael, a well-known resident of the area, was involved in the trucking. In 1927 one company, United Death Valley Clay, consolidated much of the clay production in the area. The manager, G. Ray Boggs, brought in gas-powered shovels for digging the clay, laid miles of baby-gauge rails to each pit, and put in a Plymouth locomotive and a few dozen cars to haul the clay. A processing plant powered by an old diesel submarine engine —"a constant source of grief" (Myrick, 1963:610)—was constructed at the Bradford Siding. There the clay was dried, ground, and screened prior to shipping (Lingenfelter, 1986:410; Myrick, 1963:610).

In 1928, following the closure of the borax mining operations at Ryan and the idling of the mill at Death Valley Junction, Boggs convinced the Pacific Coast Borax Company to convert the mill to handle clay. A third (baby-gauge) rail was added onto the T&T from Death Valley Junction to the Bradford Siding so that Death Valley Railroad equipment could be used to haul the clay from the pits to the mill in Death Valley Junction (Lingenfelter, 1986:410). Standard gauge was installed after 1930 (Myrick, 1963:611). The train was sent out from Death Valley Junction to pick up clay, five carloads at a time. It ran on a daily basis in later years (D. Lowe, 1988).

The mill at Death Valley Junction was powered by two diesel engines, said to have been of German manufacture. The engines generated electricity, which powered motors in the mill and also supplied electricity to the community of Death Valley Junction (Toles, 1987). At the mill the clay was first dried, then crushed. After being crushed, it was run through a Raymond mill to both grind and remove the dust. The clay was then sacked and transported to market on the T&T Railroad. The mill employed about seven men. The diesel engines typically ran from 5:00 in the morning to 11:00 at night, so the town was dark from 11:00 P.M. until 5:00 A.M.

The power plant required two operators for the two shifts. Additionally, one man ran the Raymond mill and two operated the crusher. A master mechanic and a couple of laborers worked at the bagging operation (Toles, 1987).

When there were two shifts in the pits and three in the mill, the operation turned out about 5000 tons of clay each month, worth $16 a ton in the pits and $40 a ton when processed and delivered to the refineries. United Death Valley Clay's chief backer was Fred E. Keeler, president of Lockheed Aircraft. Keeler constructed an airfield nearby so that he could drop in with one of the company planes whenever he wished (Lingenfelter, 1986:401).

Production in the Ash Meadows clay operations peaked from 1927 to 1929. Shipments ran more than 30,000 tons a year and were valued at more than $1 million annually. In 1929 Boggs left for a gold venture at Carrara and Keeler sold his interests to George W. Cohen, who renamed the operation Cohen Companies. The Depression and new developments in oil refining technology reduced demand for the clay. Production declined to 4000 tons in 1933; operations ceased when the T&T closed in 1940 (Lingenfelter, 1986:411; Toles, 1990).

Life in Clay Camp

In 1907, at about the time John Q. Lisle married Celesta Fairbanks, he located some claims in the Ash Meadows on which he believed valuable clay existed. Sometime prior to 1910, Lisle sold these claims to an oil lease company, perhaps Shell or Standard (C. Lowe, 1988). Beginning about 1918, Standard Oil began exploration for Fuller's earth (defined as any earthy material that will decolorize and brighten mineral and vegetable oils [Dymond, 1989]) in the region. Although no desirable mineral deposits were found, some open pit mining of potash took place during this period, but then was abandoned. Extensive clay mining operations began in Ash Meadows in 1923 and continued until about the time the T&T Railroad folded.

With clay mining activity in Ash Meadows increasing, John Lisle began working there for most of each winter while his family stayed in Fernley and the children attended school. After much frustration on the homestead, Lisle and his family finally abandoned Fernley in 1923 and moved to the clay camp in Ash Meadows, the newly formed community for clay mine workers and their families (C. Lowe, 1988).

Celesta Lisle Lowe, Dad Fairbanks' granddaughter, was 6 years old at the time and went to school in Clay Camp, which like so many of its predecessors on the desert was a tent town. Houses were situated along a marshy spot in Ash Meadows, perhaps just east of where the presently idled American Borite Mill stands or possibly in a spot now covered by Crystal Lake. Celesta remembers a very big pond near her house.

The tent houses of Clay Camp were appropriate for the hot, dry Nevada environment. The lower walls of the Lisle home were made of 5-gallon cans, which the family members had filled with dirt and stacked; boards were buried in the ground along the wall to help hold the cans in place. The upper portions of the tents consisted of canvas, and the interior was divided in half by a cloth partition; on one side were the beds and on the other side the living area. Boards were placed on the ground for a floor. At the end of the row of houses was a large wooden warehouse that contained the offices of the mining company (C. Lowe, 1988). There was also a wooden schoolhouse, which cost $2500 to construct. Money to build it was donated by Pan-American Oil President Edward L. Doheny (Lingenfelter, 1986:410). Lowe estimates that 12 to 15 students from the first through the eighth grades attended the school. Later the school was abandoned; the children were then transported to Death Valley Junction, after special arrangements had been made with the state of California for their education. (The schoolhouse was moved to Pahrump in 1944, where it was used until the early 1950s; currently, there is interest in properly restoring and preserving it.)

A number of small farms existed in Ash Meadows at this time, from which residents of Clay Camp purchased meat, dairy products, and fresh produce. Some farmers kept goats and pigs, and others ran cattle in the pastures. The Tubbs and the Scott families were among those living and farming in the area (C. Lowe, 1988).

Social relations within Clay Camp are remembered as warm and cordial. It was common for people to bring their suppers to each other's homes and eat together. In the evenings, residents often sat in front of their homes; at least one person would play a musical instrument and the others sang. On Sundays, residents would gather for a picnic and swim in the pool at Crystal Springs. The nearest communities were Death Valley Junction, Shoshone, and Beatty. The Lisle family usually drove to Shoshone on Saturday evening, stayed overnight, and came back Sunday. In Shoshone there was a large swimming pool, which was used year-round. South of the camp itself was another cluster of buildings, including a brothel (C. Lowe, 1988).

Richard Lingenfelter (1986:410-411) described a much more spirited community than the family-oriented camp remembered by some of its former residents, at least those who were children at the time:

> Clay City [as Lingenfelter calls it] was a "rip-roaring" camp of close to a hundred roughnecks and camp followers, who boasted that it and its surroundings were the "toughest thousand acres left of the old West." It was a hodge-podge of boardinghouses, tin shacks, and tents clustered around a

grocery store, several roadhouses offering gambling and bootleg whiskey, and a row of cribs—all bent on relieving the men of their $5.50 a day as fast as they made it. Its isolation attracted several bootleggers, who set up their stills in the surrounding brush and ran their surplus to Las Vegas at night.

Clay City prided itself in having no police, jail, preacher, or graveyard…. For all its vaunted toughness, however, the closest Clay City ever came to real violence was the suicide of a despondent prospector who hung himself in the fall of 1927, and the tragic death of a Mexican laborer the following spring.

CHAPTER 7

The Amargosa Valley
in the 1930s-1950s

uring the 1920s and 1930s, the T&T Railroad was a focal point of most activity in the Amargosa Valley. The necessities of life arrived from the outside world on its tracks; the products of the valley—clay, marble, and some agricultural products—moved south on its rails. Most valley residents depended, directly or indirectly, on the railroad for their livelihood. Moreover, the T&T was held in great affection by those in every community it served; in contrast, many residents of Las Vegas—despite a similar dependency—disliked Senator Clark's SL, LA&SP.

Stops on the T&T Railroad

In 1930, after a train left Death Valley Junction and traveled north on the T&T tracks, the first stop was Bradford Siding, just across the state border on the California side. This siding consisted of a warehouse, a relic of the Bradford Mill, including the old diesel engine, and narrow-gauge tracks leading to the clay pits. The next stops, also located in California, were Scranton and Jenifer, about which little information is available (D. Lowe, 1988).

Leeland, the first stop inside the Nevada border, was a section point just south of the Big Dune. In all, there were approximately ten sections along the T&T roadbed from Ludlow to Beatty. At Leeland, a small three- or four-room house was occupied by the section foreman and his family. This foreman was responsible for the upkeep and repair of a designated section of track along the rail line. There was also housing for the section hands and their families, consisting of four one-room units—one unit to a family. Leeland residences had dirt floors and no indoor plumbing or electricity. This was not the case at every section station on the T&T, however; but modern facilities were not available at stops in the Amargosa Valley. The section hands were nearly always immigrants from Mexico and most did not speak English. They usually did not stay more than a year or so, though a few did remain and raise families in the area. Most sent money home to Mexico regularly. The wage for a section hand was $60 a month, and it was not uncommon for a worker to send $40 or even $45 each month to Mexico in the form of a money order purchased at the express office in Death Valley Junction. The section foremen were usually Anglos, often of Irish extraction, and sometimes they did not get along with the other section foremen, at least according to some accounts. Comments like "That so-and-so down there doesn't know his business," and "He's got rough spots on the track; I've got them perfect" were heard. Section foremen were under the supervision of the roadmaster, who was responsible for the entire line, which he often traveled (D. Lowe, 1988).

After Leeland, Carrara was the next stop on the line. By the 1930s, nothing was left of the community of Gold Center, which was located just south of Beatty and was the original northern terminus of the T&T Railroad (D. Lowe, 1988).

The T&T Ranch—The Leeland Water & Land Company

For years following the completion of the T&T Railroad, the broad flat area of the Amargosa Valley lying north and west of Ash Meadows remained unoccupied. Yet experience at Leeland Station in the heart of this broad flat expanse demonstrated that the area was suitable for agriculture. Plenty of quality water was readily available from easily drilled wells, and vegetables and grain flourished in plots around the Leeland station house. Because company officials were always on the lookout for possible new sources of revenue, several trips through the area in 1914 and 1915 convinced them of the advisability of establishing an experimental farm near Leeland Station. If the agricultural productivity of the area could be proved, T&T officials reasoned, the tens of thousands of available acres in that part of the Amargosa Valley would likely fill up with homesteaders, all shipping their products on the T&T Railroad (Gower, 1969:28).

In 1915, an experimental farm, ostensibly under the direction of the University of Nevada, was established about 2 miles from Leeland Station. Harry P. Gower, a longtime employee of the Pacific Coast Borax Company, which owned the T&T Railroad, was selected as manager of the farm, with Walter Mayfield as his assistant. A couple of old shacks were moved down from Rhyolite to the farm, and months of cutting brush and clearing land began. A well was drilled, a pump installed, and a barn and corrals constructed in preparation for planting 10 acres in the spring. Because T&T officials did not know that Fordson tractors were available, two draft horses were brought to the ranch in a T&T boxcar. Gower was apparently never short on advice on how things should be done around the ranch. University of Nevada professors and Nevada politicians and their families from northern Nevada were frequently ranch guests, especially during the winter, enjoying the salubrious Amargosa winter sunshine.

The T&T Ranch operated under a succession of foremen but failed to attract other settlers to the valley because, as Gower (1969:29) said, the homestead laws were "just too tough to make it attractive in that desolate area for people of little means." Attempting to remedy that situation, company officials persuaded Nevada Senator Key Pittman to "push through Congress" legislation that enabled a U.S. citizen to acquire title to a section (640 acres) of arid Nevada desert land while continuing activities elsewhere (Gower, 1969:29). Under the terms of the 1919 legislation, an applicant could reserve four adjoining sections of "unreserved, unappropriated, nonmineral, nontimbered public lands of the United States in the State of Nevada not known to be susceptible of successful irrigation at a reasonable cost from any known source of water supply" (*The Statutes at Large* ... , 1921:293). After establishing within two years that sufficient underground water had been developed to produce a profitable agricultural crop (not native grasses) on at least 20 acres, an applicant could acquire title to one-fourth (640 acres) of the land reserved in the permit (*The Statutes at Large* ... , 1921:294).

The only homesteaders to take advantage of the legislation for the Amargosa Valley were five officials from the Pacific Coast Borax Company. They were F. M. Jenifer, F. W. Orkhill, U. S. Miller, W. W. Cahill, and C. B. Zabriskie, for whom Zabriskie Point in Death Valley is named (Records, 1987). Each claimed a section so that a large contiguous block of holdings was formed on the best land (Gower, 1969:30). The claims were eventually patented in 1927, and the deeds were signed by President Calvin Coolidge (Records, 1987). The five "homesteaders" formed the Leeland Water & Land Company; land rights were then transferred to the borax company by the owners (Gower, 1969:30; Records, 1987).

Throughout the 1930s and until the closure of the railroad, there was a fair amount of activity on the T&T Ranch. A ranch house and a few outbuildings were constructed, and a number of wells were drilled on the property, ranging from 72 to 88 feet in depth. These wells provided an abundance of water, which was pumped 24 hours a day during the peak growing season. Amargosa Valley soil was productive when watered. Alfalfa was grown, and there was a small dairy on the property. Milk and vegetables were furnished to the Furnace Creek Inn, located in Death Valley, and to the Amargosa Hotel at Death Valley Junction, both owned by the Pacific Coast Borax Company. Grapes were grown in great quantity, as were a number of fruit and nut-bearing trees. Yet despite the presence of water, good soil, sunshine, and transportation, it would be more than a decade after the closure of the railroad before serious farming activity was to begin in the Amargosa Valley outside of Ash Meadows. Of course, the slow demise of the T&T Railroad through the late 1920s and 1930s dashed all original hopes of making the Amargosa Valley an agriculturally productive area at that time.

In the late 1940s the road from Lathrop Wells to Death Valley Junction was paved. The construction company used the T&T Ranch to house some of its workers. Several buildings were brought in for the purpose and when the paving was finished the buildings remained on the property.

In about 1948 Gordon and Billie Bettles obtained an option to purchase the T&T Ranch from the Pacific Coast Borax Company. Robert J. Fishel, Billie Bettles' son, has stated that Gordon and Billie Bettles obtained the T&T Ranch about 1946 or 1947 (Fishel, 1990). Gordon Bettles was unable to execute the option's terms and in 1957 H. H. "Hank" Records, who had obtained land in the valley under the Desert Land Act, obtained an option to purchase the ranch from the borax company. Records held the ranch until 1964, when he was forced to turn it back to the Pacific Coast Borax Company. Meanwhile, Bettles continued to occupy the ranch under Records' tenure, and under the terms of the return, Bettles was allowed to keep 40 acres in gratitude for the effort he had invested in the ranch (Records, 1987).

Ash Meadows During the 1930s-1950s

The Ash Meadows area, including Death Valley Junction, continued to be the most populated section of the Amargosa Valley from the 1930s until the 1950s, although population fell significantly during the early 1930s. In 1931 approximately 100 people lived in Death Valley Junction. It was a small, face-to-face community where everyone knew everyone else. Death Valley Junction was a company town owned by the Pacific Coast Borax Company, and no saloons or dance halls were permitted (Toles, 1987).

All supplies and mail came into Death Valley Junction by rail—either on the T&T or on the Gallopin' Goose, an odd-looking railroad vehicle consisting of a gas-electric engine and one coach. Herb Toles, who was not yet 20 years old, moved to Death Valley Junction in 1931, preceded by his uncle and grandfather, who worked in the clay pits. Herb operated the "candy wagon" in town. This was a delivery wagon that transported to the town's residents all types of supplies, including ice, which came from the town's own ice plant. Mail reached Furnace Creek through regular truck service down Furnace Creek Wash.

Harry P. Gower was the on-site boss of the Pacific Coast Borax Company, which operated the mill at Death Valley

Junction. The town virtually closed down for 3 months every summer due to the heat; the mill was closed and few services were available. Only four or five people remained in town at this time, including the storekeeper, a man to manage the power plant, and an agent at the railroad station to look after the telegraph and relay messages to Furnace Creek (D. Lowe, 1988).

Old-timers remember at least three clay pits in Ash Meadows in the early 1930s. One, the Bell Pit, was located just to the south of the current American Borate Corporation (ABC) mill. A second, the Associated Pit, was south and west of the Bell Pit. Additionally, the Ballingers, father and son, had operated a clay pit and a small mill about 3 miles out into Ash Meadows west of the present site of the ABC mill. Toles remembered that there was still a diesel engine at the Bradford Mill at Bradford Siding in 1931, although the mill was not functioning (its operations had been transferred to Death Valley Junction).

In 1931, Cohen Companies operated the Bell Pit. The Associated and Ballinger pits had by this time closed. The clay at the Bell Pit was mined by means of a drag line and it was loaded directly into rail cars on the baby-gauge spur rail line. These cars were hauled up a ramp, where the clay was dumped into cars on the T&T spur to the Ash Meadows clay pits. Approximately five men worked at the site: four men operated the drag line and the baby-gauge rail, and one was the superintendent (Toles, 1990).

Clay Camp was on its last legs by the early 1930s. The tent houses from the peak production days were gone. Two large buildings remained: a bunkhouse built from railroad ties for the workers and a frame house that provided living quarters for the superintendent and his family. A recreation hall, which the Associated Oil Company had previously built, was located nearby. During the 1930s there was a saloon and brothel near the Ballinger Clay Pit. An old schoolhouse was also located nearby, and dances were regularly held in the building. Many of those who came to the dances were from Death Valley Junction, which was a company town and had no saloon or dance hall (Toles, 1987). Other structures in Ash Meadows in 1931 included buildings on the Bradford, Tubbs, and Staley homesteads. Jack Pardee and Jepperson had homes in the area. Pete Peterson arrived in 1934. The McCalls occupied the so-called Jap Ranch, which was said to have been named after a man whose nickname was Jap but who was not Japanese (Toles, 1990).

The Ash Meadows Lodge was constructed in about 1933 or 1934. Its builder was a young man from Los Angeles by the name of Berry, who was backed by what were apparently some well-endowed financial sources. The Ash Meadows Lodge catered to tourists from southern California and was a favored eating place for the residents of Death Valley Junction. Berry sold out about the time the T&T Railroad shut down. In 1948 Jessie Windsor began using the property, and in 1950 Francis D'Albertin Sticht was declared the legal owner following a lawsuit ("Sticht Wins Decision in Ash Meadows Suit," 1950). The property reopened in the 1950s as a brothel after nuclear weapons testing began at the Nevada Test Site, and an airstrip was built near the rancho to accommodate clients. Meanwhile, small-scale ranching continued in Ash Meadows, with the Tubbs family, among others, remaining there.

Lathrop Wells, 1930-1950

In 1931 the only activity at what would later be called Lathrop Wells was a State of Nevada highway maintenance station. The first of the present two saloons was not constructed until about 1948. During the early 1950s, William

Lear constructed a runway at Lathrop Wells and tested early versions of his Lear Jet (Toles, 1987). In the middle 1980s Lathrop Wells' name was changed to Amargosa Valley as much of the Amargosa Valley was incorporated into the unincorporated town of Amargosa Valley.

Carrara and the Marble Quarry

The town of Carrara was founded in 1912 on the northeastern edge of the Amargosa Valley, three miles down the mountain from the newly formed American Carrara Marble Company quarry. About 40 buildings were laid out near the LV&T tracks. The town's central attraction was a marble fountain, 18 feet across and 3 feet deep, with a 6-foot column of water piped from Gold Center—9 miles away (Myrick, 1963:605-606).

The quarry was named after the famous marble obtained in the mountains of Carrara, Italy. Operations peaked between 1915 and 1916, when about 60 men were on the company payroll. However, operations ceased in 1916 because electrical service was abruptly halted. The company had faced increased competition from Vermont marble and artificial marble tiles (Myrick, 1963:606-607).

Operations were briefly revived in 1927, and it was necessary to construct a 3/4-mile spur from the T&T Railroad to Carrara since the LV&T Railroad had folded earlier (Myrick, 1963:607). Nevertheless, during the early 1930s, Carrara was described as "a nice little town." Company offices and homes constructed of wood lined a straight road that led up to the marble quarry, and the marble fountain still attracted the attention of visitors (Colvin, 1987).

About 1940 a member of the Elizalde family (a Filipino family involved in the hemp business) became interested in Carrara. The young man, an engineer, intended to use the stone to make colored cement. Although by now both the LV&T and the T&T railroads had ceased operating, a mill was constructed. A clay dryer from the mill at Death Valley Junction was moved overland to Carrara. However, the mill never became operational. After Pearl Harbor and the beginning of World War II, the Filipino investors who supported the venture backed out and the operation ceased (Toles, 1987).

P. V. Perkins, the founder of the American Carrara Marble Company, died in Kentucky in 1955 at the age of 70. It is said that his marble venture brought in excess of $1 million into the local economy ("Carrara Founder Dies in Kentucky," 1955).

CHAPTER 8

Modern Development of the Amargosa Valley

he modern era of Amargosa Valley development really began in the early 1950s, when the federal government opened the valley to settlement under the terms of the Desert Land Act, which passed in 1877 and was amended in 1891 and 1915 (Nevada Department of Conservation and Natural Resources, 1985). Prior to that time, the only people living in the Amargosa Valley resided in Lathrop Wells and the Ash Meadows area. Closure of the T&T Railroad left the T&T Ranch "high and dry," as Harry P. Gower (1969:30) put it, and the property was abandoned about the time of World War II and remained unoccupied until Gordon and Billie Bettles moved onto the property around 1948. Not long afterward, Hank and Robert Records took up residence nearby.

Gordon and Billie Bettles on the T&T Ranch

Gordon Bettles was born in 1893 in Helena, Montana. When Gordon was 13, his mother died and his father moved with Gordon and two other sons, Alex and A. J., to Sodaville,

Nevada, located a few miles south of Mina on U.S. Highway 95. Gordon and his younger brother Alex attended a military school in San Francisco, from which they graduated. Bettles attended the University of Nevada for a time, married, worked as a truck driver, and while still in his early twenties, returned to Mina. Bettles' first wife died during the flu epidemic of 1918 after the birth of their second child, Helen. Described by relatives as a "lady's man," Bettles married five times, had a pioneering spirit, and enjoyed new situations (Brockman, 1987).

He met his fifth wife, Billie, at the clay camp in Ash Meadows (Records, 1990). Billie, whose given name was Willie Odetta McElrath, was born in 1901 in Coleman, Texas, located south of Abilene, Texas. Billie and Gordon were married in Tonopah in about 1927. Together they operated a cleaning business in Hawthorne, Nevada; in 1935 they moved to Fernley, where they ranched, and where Gordon served as a justice of the peace. In 1940 they moved to Reno, where they operated a wholesale cleaning business (Brockman, 1987). While in Reno, Billie Bettles suffered an illness similar to a stroke, perhaps even polio.

The Bettles spent a number of months in Tecopa, California, so Billie could soak in the hot springs. They found the people friendly and enjoyed the climate and desert environment (Brockman, 1987).

Bettles was a gregarious man who knew people throughout the state because he habitually stopped at diners for coffee while traveling. His natural friendliness led him to make many acquaintances. Bettles, who had previously met Harry P. Gower, discussed with him the possible acquisition of the T&T Ranch. While Billie was recuperating, Gordon obtained an option to purchase the T&T. Bettles encouraged his oldest daughter, Edith Brockman, and her husband, Frank, who then lived in Bishop, California, to take a piece of the T&T Ranch. The Brockmans, however, were advised by a California agricultural agent they knew in Bishop that any land that grew creosote would not support agricultural products (Brockman, 1987).

In fact, nothing but creosote was growing on the ranch when the Bettles first moved there in the late 1940s. Gordon and Billie were the only residents in the Amargosa farm area; the Brockmans remember the Bettles' place as being quite spartan in the first years. Most of the trees and grape vineyards that had been planted on the T&T years earlier were dead. Gordon and Billie constructed a home from a tall, faded orange building that had once housed railroad workers, which they moved in from Death Valley Junction (Fishel, 1990). Around the house, Billie, who was a master gardener, created a garden about 200 to 300 feet wide full of trees, flowers, and vegetables (Brockman, 1987). They grew a wide variety of plants. The most important crop was alfalfa, but corn was also grown. Both crops were sold locally and in Las Vegas. Bettles held an option on the farm land, and he used the lovely alfalfa fields as a promotion to interest others in the area. To water the fields, he used a flood-irrigation system of siphon tubes, which had to be moved every 2-1/2 hours. The water was pumped by diesel engines that ran continuously.

After the Bettles had been on the T&T Ranch for a few years, Pat and M. P. "Gles" Glessner, Billie's daughter and son-in-law, acquired 5 acres of Desert Land Act property at the junction of Mecca Road and the Lathrop Wells-Death Valley Junction highway. Beginning about 1955 or 1956, the Glessners built a home there. It had been their intention to retire in the area, but their plans changed. The Bettles acquired the property from the Glessners and moved from the T&T Ranch to the house on Mecca Road. In 1962 Bettles began con-

struction of a building nearby that eventually housed the
Mecca Club, but he died before he could complete it. Billie
Bettles stayed on in the Amargosa Valley for a number of
years and then moved to the Pahrump Valley. Bettles'
daughter, Edith, stated that Gordon, a member of the
Masonic Lodge, seemed to have derived his greatest satisfac-
tion in life from participation in Masonic activities (Brockman,
1987).

Modern Pioneers: The Records Brothers

Hank Records and his brother, Robert, were among the
first to take advantage of new opportunities to claim land in
the valley under the Desert Land Act. Hank Records was born
in New Mexico in 1918 and spent much of his youth in
southern Colorado. As a young man he moved to California,
where he mined and worked in the oil fields. During World
War II, he was an officer with the 1884th Aviation Engineer
Battalion. He served with the battalion at Tulagi, the Solomon
Islands, and Palau in the South Pacific, and he helped construct the runway at Guam from which large numbers of B-29s
took off to bomb Japan (Records, 1987, 1990).

Following the war Hank mined in Arizona, and in 1950 he
helped develop a mine near the Ubehebe Crater in Death
Valley. In 1950, Hank and Robert were consulting in Beatty.
They returned to Death Valley by way of Highway 129 (now
Highway 373) that connected Lathrop Wells and Death Valley
Junction. As they drove across the Amargosa Valley they were
struck by its broad, beautiful expanse. "That beautiful flat
valley," Hank exclaimed. "Something should be done with
it." Years later brother Robert jokingly commented, "That's
when they should've put us in a straitjacket." Having grown
up on a farm, both men appreciated the value and potential of
good, flat agricultural land. At the time, the only occupants of

the valley besides the settlers in Ash Meadows (including the Tubbs, Rookers, and Pete Peterson) and a few families in Death Valley Junction were the Bettles, who lived on the T&T Ranch. Lathrop Wells consisted only of a service station on the north side of the highway, owned by Harry Petting, and the Shamrock brothel, located somewhat behind and to the east of the service station (Records, 1987).

Hank and Robert immediately looked into the possibilities of farming in the Amargosa Valley, and upon discovering that land was available under the Desert Land Act, made a quick trip to Carson City to obtain the necessary papers. The Desert Land Act was designed to enable people to make habitable and take title to highly arid land; the terms were different than those of the Homestead Act. Under the Desert Land Act a person was allowed to claim 320 acres. In order to take title, one had to drill wells and prove enough water for the entire 320 acres, plant a total of 40 acres, and pay the federal government $1.25 per acre. Noting where the T&T wells were located and knowing the shallow depth of the wells, Hank and Robert and their families staked out Sections 24 and 19, while a friend took Section 18. The Records brothers were the first to officially file in the valley under the Desert Land Act (Records, 1987).

In 1953, the brothers returned to the Amargosa Valley with $30,000 and began drilling wells. They moved into trailer homes, began to clear the creosote brush from the land, brought in pumps and irrigation rigs, and then planted alfalfa and wheat. The brothers grew wheat and alfalfa in the early years and sold the alfalfa locally, mainly at the Furnace Creek Inn. They were able to obtain six cuttings of alfalfa a year, and they also raised replacement cows for the Jessop Dairy in Los Angeles. In the next few years they experimented with potatoes and other crops, including cantaloupes, watermelon, peanuts, and onions. In their efforts to develop agriculture in the valley, Hank, Robert, and the other pioneers who followed relied on any solid sources of information they could find—seed companies, state officials, university experts, and others. Alfalfa was and remains the mainstay of agriculture in the valley, although experimentation continues, lately in pistachios and peaches. Alfalfa is especially good for the soil because it binds nitrogen and provides richer growing conditions for crops that may be planted later (Records, 1987).

The Records brothers were followed into what is now known in the valley as the Farm Area by the Mankinens, the Stricklands, and the Selbachs. Many of the later arrivals, including the Stricklands and Selbachs, supplemented farming with employment at the Nevada Test Site. In 1956, Hank Records purchased the old T&T Ranch for $37.50 an acre; he held it until 1960. In subsequent years the original five sections of the T&T were sold off in parcels and by 1988 little more than half of the original land was held by a single owner (Records, 1987).

Modern Pioneer Hardships

The first modern settlers in the valley, like their predecessors, endured many hardships. One of the most serious, especially during the first years, was the lack of roads. The network of paved highways that now crisscrosses the valley is a far cry from what Hank Records and the other pioneers first encountered. When the T&T was the only ranch in the farm area of the valley, the roads led out in straight lines like spokes of a wheel from the T&T Ranch to Death Valley Junction, Lathrop Wells, and Highway 95. As farming activity increased, the farmers made their own roads by pulling a small grader behind a tractor, uprooting creosote bushes along the way. These crude roads, which tended to follow section lines, were very dusty and it was not uncommon to literally get stuck in the dust (Records, 1987).

Electric service was not available in the Amargosa Valley even as recently as 1963. Each water well had to have its own pump and motor, and the motors often ran nearly continuously. Hank Records, for instance, used a GMC diesel engine at each well to power the pump. Maintenance and upkeep were constant problems, and costs were higher than comparable electric equipment. Unless one was willing to run a small generator all summer, an electric fan at home could be a luxury; modern air conditioning was unavailable, although some people did operate swamp coolers for part of the day or night. Unless one had a gas-operated refrigerator (a Servel) there was no hope of continuous refrigeration and the consequent convenience, perhaps necessity, of ice and cold foods. Food was kept cool in a barrel covered with wet gunny sacks. If the sacks dried out, things would spoil rapidly and butter would liquify in the summer heat (Records, 1987).

Amargosa Valley winds, which tend to blow either from the north or the south, can be severe. One resident called the Amargosa Valley the "valley of blowing rocks" in reference to the 35- to 40-mile per hour winds that seem almost strong enough to pick up rocks. Winds can be an especially bad problem when the soil is first broken because there are no trees and there is little or no blacktop, as was the case when farming first got started in the 1950s (Records, 1987; Boyd, 1987).

Late frosts can also be a problem in the valley. Trees bud in February, but one in four years there is a killing frost in March. Such frosts can nip early alfalfa shoots and retard plant growth. Freezing pipes and pumps were, and still can be, serious problems. Farmers such as Hank Records run their pumps and run water through the pipes when the water temperature drops. Because the water emerges from the wells at 74 degrees, freezing is prevented (Records, 1987).

Obtaining parts and repairs on farm equipment and vehicles was difficult in the early years and remains so. At that time, Las Vegas was a small community that was not oriented toward agriculture. Hank Records and the other pioneers had to think of Lancaster, California, nearly 200 miles away, as their parts and supply center. When equipment broke down or a vital part was needed, it was necessary to either drive to Lancaster to obtain the part, order it by mail (with mail pickup at Lathrop Wells), or, in some cases, have dealers fly badly needed parts into the valley; they landed on the old dirt roads (Records, 1987).

Another problem for Amargosa Valley farmers—one that has not been fully solved to this day—is finding a market for their products. Although water abounds and the soil is fertile, and virtually anything that grows will thrive, the nearest market is Las Vegas—which until recent years was relatively small. The next market of any size is the Los Angeles area, and it is nearly 300 miles to the harbor at San Pedro. Valley farmers have found that growers of food products are often locked into long-term contracts with buyers and must guarantee high volume. It is difficult for farmers to break into such contracting agreements, especially those on a geographic margin such as the Amargosa Valley. Moreover, it is hard for small farmers to guarantee buyers large volumes of produce early in the development of their farms. An Amargosa farmer may be able to supply a buyer with a few products such as tomatoes and potatoes at a competitive price, but usually a buyer is already committed to arrangements with other suppliers who produce many more crops than just potatoes or tomatoes. Thus, the buyer is reluctant to purchase products from the Amargosa farmer because this might jeopardize the business relationship with the larger supplier. The independent nature of farmers and the resulting difficulties people have experienced in attempting to form farmers' cooperatives in the valley have added to the marketing problem (Records, 1987).

As if these problems were not enough, there was also the difficulty the first settlers of the farm area experienced in maintaining families in the valley during the early years. The spartan and pioneer conditions, in contrast to most parts of the United States in the middle of the twentieth century, were not to the liking of many women. As a result, household composition during this period was mostly male; men left their wives and children in cities such as Los Angeles and only visited them periodically (Records, 1987).

The hardships faced by Amargosa Valley pioneers discouraged many who gave up and moved away. Old-timers have noticed that it often took a series of individuals to develop a farm. A pioneering person would come in, develop a farm to a point, and become discouraged or go broke, and leave; that person was followed by another farmer who made some additions and improvements to the place, only to become discouraged or broke. The process continued until a farm was fully developed and economically operated (Records, 1987).

In recent years, Amargosa Valley farmers have had to contend with new problems; unlike those produced by nature in the past, these problems are man-made and result from current perceptions of the world. Though the land and water claims of farmers like Hank and Robert Records date back more than 30 years, there is an effort by Nevada state water officials to restrict Amargosa farmers from pumping groundwater. If successful, these efforts will spell the end of farming in the western part of the valley, as surely as it has ceased in the Ash Meadows area. Valley farmers believe state actions are unfair and are based on minimal hydrological information. They see state officials, however well-intentioned, as acting like czars, disregarding empirical evidence and local concerns. The state's alleged reason for restricting groundwater pumping for agriculture is to preserve groundwater resources beneath the valley. The farmers point out that the original well on the T&T Ranch, drilled more than 50 years ago, has not dropped more than 3 or 4 feet despite all the pumping during the past 30 years. Many Amargosa Valley residents believe that the restriction of water pumping in the valley is the first step in a long-term attempt by the state to expropriate groundwater resources in the valley for delivery to the thirsty city of Las Vegas.

Valley farmers also feel victimized by the federal government's policy of preservation of wild horses. Large numbers of these animals reside in the Amargosa Valley and are free to range on farmers' fields. Though farmers protest loudly to county, state, and federal government officials, there is little relief. Even when horses are removed, they return within a few years. In 1987, 28 wild horses poached on Hank Records' alfalfa fields, and he was unable to do anything about it. At a public meeting one wild-horse supporter suggested Records should fence his field. He replied, "If I had the money for that, I would retire" (Records, 1987).

Electricity in the Amargosa Valley

Amargosa Valley residents tried for years to interest the Nevada Power Company in extending service to the valley but they were always told that the cost was prohibitive. "They wanted $69,000 just to extend power to the T&T [Ranch] and that was if everyone in the country signed up, too" (Sternberg, 1986:2). One evening in 1960, while sitting at their kitchen table, Hank and Robert Records decided to try to form an electric cooperative. They discussed the ideas with valley residents Ed Mankinen, Ralph Dalton, and Gene Eastabrooks and soon formed a nonprofit corporation: the Amargosa Valley Electric Cooperative. Hank Records then contacted Department of Interior officials in Washington, D.C., and officials from the Rural Electrification Administration (REA). Records realized that political clout and a strong case would be needed to demonstrate the community's need for electric power. He contacted officials at the Nevada Test Site and convinced them that the giant defense facility should have a backup supply of power in addition to that provided by the Nevada Power Company. Records then began signing up prospective customers in the Amargosa Valley. In the meantime, he lined up an engineering firm from Albuquerque, New Mexico, to conduct a feasibility study; he personally guaranteed its labor costs if the effort failed. At the same time, residents in Pahrump formed an electric cooperative, the Pahrump Valley Utility Company; both groups were advised that a merger would increase their chances of getting power so the two entities joined forces (Records, 1987). Ralph Dalton and Robert Records stepped down from the board of directors, and Elmer Bowman and Walt Williams from Pahrump became members (Records, 1989).

By now, the effort was beginning to meet formal resistance from both the Nevada Power Company and from Southern California Edison across the border in California (Records, 1987). Both were jealously guarding what they perceived as their jurisdiction. Southern California Edison was upset because the cooperative intended to provide power to Furnace Creek and Death Valley Junction. "Southern California Edison would have us in court in Los Angeles on one day and Nevada Power Company would have us in court in Tonopah the next. All we could do was hire attorneys to represent us," Records remembered (Sternberg, 1986:4). Moreover, the giant power companies did not confine themselves only to legal action. Recognizing they might be outdone by newcomers, the Nevada Power Company began constructing "spite lines" into the Amargosa Valley and at one point ran the power poles up to Hank Records' property line. The poles were quickly sawed down in the dark of night; the identity of the culprit was never ascertained (Records, 1987). Southern California Edison, meanwhile, hooked up everyone on their side of the state line—areas such as Death Valley—dashing the cooperative's hopes of bringing power there (Sternberg, 1986:3).

Though they met with considerable resistance from the Nevada Power Company and Southern California Edison, the cooperative, with Hank Records spearheading the effort, secured 10,000 kilowatts of power from Davis Dam on the lower Colorado River. However, the cooperative soon realized that it would be too expensive to bring power from Davis Dam to the Amargosa Valley; when members learned that Hoover Dam power was fully allotted, a trade was arranged with an Arizona power company that held rights to Hoover Dam power. The Arizona company took over Amargosa's rights at Davis Dam, and the Amargosa Valley Electric Cooperative acquired rights to 10,000 kilowatts of power from Hoover Dam (Records, 1987).

Eventually, a loan was secured with the help of the National Rural Electric Cooperative Association. Hank Records was instrumental in bringing that group's annual convention to Las Vegas in 1963, and at a session of the convention he made the case for power for Amargosa Valley and Pahrump. Soon thereafter, loan money became available through the REA, and power lines were strung from Hoover Dam across the Las Vegas Valley, over the Spring Mountains, and into Pahrump. From Pahrump the lines went to the Amargosa Valley, then on to Beatty and Sarcobatus Flat. Power for Fish

Lake Valley was arranged through a trade with California power sources. Additionally, a line was furnished to Death Valley Scotty's Castle across the border in California from Sarcobatus Flat. The cooperative also supplied power to the Nevada state line, at which point it was picked up by Southern California Edison and distributed to Death Valley Junction and Furnace Creek. Power was turned on in the Amargosa Valley in 1963. The advent of economical electric power in the Amargosa helped initiate a new era of development. Afford-able electricity substantially reduced the cost of pumping water and made the area more attractive for people to build residences and to operate farms (Records, 1987).

Gordon Bettles had been active with Hank Records and others in securing electric power for the Amargosa Valley. Ironically, Bettles' funeral services in Beatty were conducted on the day power was turned on in Lathrop Wells. His body was transported to Las Vegas after the services. When the funeral procession passed through Lathrop Wells, the lights in that community were dimmed in tribute to Gordon Bettles (Brockman, 1987).

Law Enforcement in the Amargosa Valley

The vast stretches of Nye County have always been a challenge for law enforcement. From its first days of settle-ment until well into the 1930s, Ash Meadows was considered a dangerous and inhospitable place for strangers, and espe-cially lawmen. Yet the vast distances in Nye County and the unpretentious character of social relationships among its widely dispersed residents also created opportunities for the formation of special bonds between lawmen and those they served. Most recognized the need for effective law enforce-ment and respected the lawman who did his job well. Sheriff William H. Thomas was one such man. The former owner of a meat market in Tonopah, he served as sheriff of Nye County from the time of World War I until the 1950s. He seldom wore a gun or resorted to physical force and was respected and loved throughout the county.

Robert Revert, who served as deputy sheriff in charge of southern Nye County from 1946 to 1960, was another highly regarded lawman. When he was first elected, Sheriff Thomas cautioned him, "You'll have no soft time of it. I consider Ash Meadows to be the worst part of this county" for law enforcement (Revert, 1988). Indeed, during Prohibition Ash Meadows was openly full of bootleggers. Celesta Lowe remembered that people drove to Ash Meadows from Beatty, Death Valley Junction, Shoshone, Furnace Creek, and even Las Vegas to buy moonshine (C. Lowe, 1988). During that era one federal agent disappeared in Ash Meadows. His car was recovered, but his body was never found (Revert, 1988).

Modern Mining
of Amargosa Valley Clays

Following the closure of the Ash Meadows clay camp one year prior to World War II, exploration of the Amargosa Valley clay deposits by a number of individuals continued. In the 1960s, brothers W. Howard Prescott, Jr., and Edward P. Prescott formed a partnership. The Prescotts had been involved in the production of taconite in the iron ore business, and they were familiar with the uses of bentonite clay in the smelting of iron ore. A man named Ewing had earlier acquired a number of claims on clay deposits in the valley, and the Prescotts acquired these as well as claims controlled by the Cappaert Ranch in Ash Meadows. The Ewing bentonite pit near the dry lake at the far eastern edge of the Amargosa Valley, near the present community of Crystal, is named after Ewing. In 1972 the Prescott partnership became incorporated, forming Industrial Mineral Ventures, Inc. (IMV). At first the company was headquartered in Golden, Colorado, but it later moved its offices to Las Vegas. In 1977 IMV was acquired by Gulf Resources and Chemical Corporation of Houston, Texas (Hansen, 1987).

Though the Amargosa Valley contains vast deposits of commercially valuable clay, including some forms found nowhere else in the world, IMV's early efforts at refining were not very successful. The turning point came when it was discovered that the clays could be processed through extrusion. When the clays are extruded under high pressure through small holes in a die (not unlike the process of pressing pasta dough through a form nozzle), the small clay particles are sheared from one another, resulting in a high-quality product. Before 1978, when the extrusion processing techniques were mastered, IMV employed as many as 125 workers in the Amargosa Valley, including 22 in the lab. Many workers lived in the valley, although some resided in Shoshone and Pahrump. With increased efficiency, by 1985 the same productivity level was attained with 55-60 workers, with most living in the Amargosa Valley. Prior to 1980, IMV experienced a high rate of turnover among its employees, but increased efficiency and the advent of economic hard times nationally contributed to a relatively low turnover rate in the early 1980s (Hansen, 1987).

IMV mines several different kinds of clay. Most of their mining operations are located near the Ewing pit at the eastern edge of the valley. Other IMV clay pits are found west of the mill site, which is located 15 miles south of the Lathrop Wells-Death Valley Junction highway and 2 miles west on a dirt access road. Sepiolite, hectorite, and smectites are among the clays mined by IMV. Very high quality sepiolite is known as meerschaum. IMV's sepiolite deposit in the Amargosa Valley is the only known one in the United States. These salt-tolerant clays are used in drilling in the presence of salt water; for example, in an underground salt dome. (When drilling, clay is circulated in the drill hole under extremely high pressure, sealing off cracks in the drill hole. The circulating clay also removes the cuttings from the hole [Potts, 1989].) The sepiolite clays also are used in the manufacture of asphalt, roofing compounds, tape joint cement, stucco, latex, and spackling compounds. In Japan, IMV's sepiolites are used as an asbestos replacement. IMV holds the rights to hundreds of thousands of tons of sepiolite in the Amargosa Valley (Hansen, 1987).

Hectorite, another type of clay mined by IMV in the Amargosa Valley, makes up only 5 percent of the total clay produced but accounts for 60 percent of IMV's profits (Hansen, 1987). At IMV, hectorite is processed with a compound that includes steer fat and alcohol. In the process, the clay changes from a hydroscopic clay—a clay that attracts water—to a hydrophobic clay, one that rejects water. In effect, the inorganic clay molecule is coated with an organic one during processing. The organoclad clays (as they are called) produced by IMV are used in paints, greases, and plastics. Organoclad clays are also used when drillers hit oil because the drilling compounds must be compatible with the oil and not antagonistic as they are with water. Organoclad clays are also used to coat candies such as M&Ms (Hansen, 1987).

Smectite, the third type of clay processed by IMV, expands in the presence of water. If a couple of tablespoons of bentonite, a smectite clay, are added to a glass of water, the glass will be filled with a thick gel by the next morning because the clay expands and absorbs the water. The addition of soda ash increases the swelling capacity. IMV combines bentonite with saponite; the product is used as drilling fluid, in stucco wall and ceiling coatings, and as a filler and sealant in the burial of chemical waste (Hansen, 1987).

In the late 1980s IMV produced about 35,000 to 40,000 tons of clays annually in the Amargosa Valley; the company owns or controls about 45,000 acres, most of it in the valley, but some in California. Approximately 5000 acres are patented claims. The IMV plant is the Amargosa Valley's most important economic resource (Hansen, 1987).

Another clay mining operation, which is very small by comparison, is located just west of the IMV plant at the base of the Funeral Mountains. This clay mine, known as the Vanderbilt Mine, is the source of very fine-grained clays that are processed and sold by the pound to cosmetic producers. A smile comes to Amargosa Valley residents when they consider that people around the world wear a bit of the Amargosa Valley on their faces when attempting to look their very best (Hansen, 1987; Jackson, 1987).

American Borate Company in the Amargosa Valley

In the early 1970s, Tenneco began operating a borax processing facility in the Amargosa Valley. Initially, colemanite, a calcium borate (borax) ore named for William T. Coleman, was obtained in an open pit mine, the Billy Mine, near Furnace Creek Wash, approximately halfway between Death Valley Junction and the Furnace Creek Inn in Death Valley. California environmental laws restricted construction of a processing plant in California, so a borax processing facility was built in the Amargosa Valley just across the Nevada border. The Billy Mine, which was located within the borders of the Death Valley National Monument, became depleted and the company was forced to mine the colemanite through underground mining techniques. A deep shaft was sunk outside of the national monument, and the colemanite ore was removed from the mine and trucked to the mill on the edge of Ash

Meadows. Tenneco operated the mine and mill until about 1976, when it was sold to the American Borate Company (ABC) (Hansen, 1987; Jackson, 1987, 1989).

Two communities were constructed to house the mine and mill workers. One was located on the California side of the border in Furnace Creek Wash not far from the mine. It contained about 50 mobile homes and was known as the Valley Crest Park. The second community was constructed on the Nevada side of the border just south of the ABC mill near the Stateline Saloon. Known as the Stateline Trailer Park, it consisted of approximately 100 mobile homes. Additionally, many workers lived in mobile homes out in the valley on lots or small acreages. Other workers lived in Shoshone, Furnace Creek, and Pahrump, with a few commuting from as far away as Beatty. Between 1981 and 1983, employment at the mine and mill climbed to almost 500 workers. The mine's profitability, however, was adversely affected by the importation of colemanite products from Turkey at prices lower than production costs at the Amargosa Valley operation (Jackson, 1987, 1989). The American Borate Company closed the entire operation in April 1986.

ABC's operation had contributed substantially to the economy of the Amargosa Valley. The additional population from the mine and mill, and subsidies from ABC, led to the development of the small shopping center at the intersection of Mecca Road and the Lathrop Wells-Death Valley Junction highway. A number of apartment units were built behind the shopping center to house company workers. A restaurant was opened just west of the Stateline Saloon and a branch of the Valley Bank was established nearby. Doris Jackson expanded the Stateline Saloon, located just south of the Stateline Trailer Park, partly to accommodate the hard-working, hard-living miners. Under her management the

Saloon became a community gathering place, where women, children, and even dogs were assured of courteous treatment. Nevada-style gaming and live music on Friday and Saturday nights were available (Jackson, 1987).

Peat Mining the Carson Slough

Man and habitat had coexisted for unknown scores of centuries in Ash Meadows without controversy. But all that began to change in the early 1960s when for three years the Carson Slough was mined for peat. When the mining was completed, bordering sand dunes were graded into the now-dry slough and mixed with the lower grade of peat that remained. The operation converted a large wetland area into dry agricultural fields, destroying a habitat for many species of aquatic insects, fish, and other animals and eliminating a "major wintering stop for waterfowl and other migratory birds" (Cook and Williams, 1982:IV-2), and depriving the state of one of its finest waterfowl hunting areas (Cook and Williams, 1982:V-13). Mining of the slough represented a significant degradation of the Ash Meadows environment and was followed by a controversial and, as it turned out, legally unacceptable first effort at large-scale agricultural development of Ash Meadows.

The Spring Meadows Ranch and the Pupfish Controversy

Prior to the late 1960s no real effort to practice agriculture in the Ash Meadows area on a large scale had been made. Residents historically practiced small-scale production, and most of the land remained under the jurisdiction of the Bureau of Land Management. Then, in the late 1960s, Spring Meadows, Inc., exchanged 5400 acres in the Osgood Mountains for 5645 acres in Ash Meadows (Cook and Williams, 1982:I-1).

Through additional purchases of private holdings in Ash Meadows, Spring Meadows, Inc., increased its holdings to 12,000 acres and garnered the majority of the area's water rights. Wells were drilled and the pumping of water began with an extensive irrigation system. The establishment of a large cattle operation provided jobs for more than 100 workers. As one resident described it, "They ran cattle and horses and raised alfalfa and all their own feed" (Jackson, 1987).

Prior to this, about the time of the mining of the Carson Slough, naturalists had become interested in the area; in particular, biologists examined a number of species said to be endemic to Ash Meadows. Experts contended that the incidence of endemic North American plants and animals in Ash Meadows was second only to a locale in central Mexico (Cook and Williams, 1982:II-4). Of special concern were a number of dwarf fish species known as pupfish, in particular the so-called Devils Hole pupfish. It was known to reside only in Devils Hole and was readily identifiable by its small size, lack of pelvic fins, and by a dorsal fin placed far back on its spine. The Devils Hole pupfish was thought to have lived in isolation for thousands of years, since the Great Basin began drying up about 10,000 years ago. Other distinct and endangered species of pupfish found in Ash Meadows include several varieties of the Warm Springs pupfish and the Ash Meadows pupfish; another fish from there, a minnow known as the Ash Meadows speckled dace, is also endangered.

Other endemic species in Ash Meadows include a beetle, a snail, and several plants, including two from the sunflower family and one each from the goosefoot, pea, loasa, and rose families (Cook and Williams, 1982:Chapter II). The controversy, however, centered on the Devils Hole pupfish. (In mute testimony to early residents' opinion of the Ash Meadows pupfish, one of Dad Fairbanks' daughter's favorite pastimes was to catch them and feed them to her cat.)

In 1952, President Harry Truman proclaimed Devils Hole a disjunct part of the Death Valley National Monument (Cook and Williams, 1982:IV-1). In 1962 the National Park Service installed a device for measuring water-level fluctuations in Devils Hole in anticipation of future agricultural developments (Cook and Williams, 1982:IV-2). As water pumping associated with ranching in Ash Meadows increased in the late 1960s and into the 1970s, water levels in Devils Hole and other springs in the meadows dropped, and many naturalists contended that endangered species were being further threatened. The controversy between the naturalists and ranching interests ended up in court, and on June 7, 1976, the U.S. Supreme Court stated that the government had the right to maintain water levels in Devils Hole because it was a part of the Death Valley National Monument. In 1978 a minimum allowable level of water was established in Devils Hole (Cook and Williams, 1982:IV-2-3).

As a result of these decisions, the Spring Meadows Ranch was put up for sale. "They had a bankruptcy sale. They probably [had] a mile of just farm equipment that they auctioned off. They sold the trailers the workers lived in. Many of the employees, many of whom were Mexicans, found other jobs in the Valley, some at IMV" (Jackson, 1987). The ranch initially was offered to the U.S. Fish and Wildlife Service, and though the State of Nevada offered to share in the cost of the ranch's purchase, the offer was turned down. Naturalists say that the federal government had failed to realize the large number of threatened and endangered species in addition to the Devils Hole pupfish in Ash Meadows at this time (Cook and Williams, 1982:IV-3). Consequently, in 1980 the Spring Meadows Ranch was sold to Preferred Equities, a land development company based in Pahrump. Preferred Equities made additional purchases of land in Ash Meadows, bringing its total ownership to about 17,000 acres. The land development company moved forward with plans to subdivide its holdings in Ash Meadows; it anticipated the eventual development of 33,600 lots and a community of 50,000. Environmentalists learned of the plans, and a move was mounted to block further development. The Nature Conservancy, the National Wildlife Federation, the Audubon Society, and the Sierra Club were active in efforts to stop Preferred Equities (Cook and Williams, 1982:IV-4-5).

A number of plans were offered for the "preservation" of the Ash Meadows area (Cook and Williams, 1982:VI; Sada, 1984:19-40). Initially, there was an attempt to arrange a land swap between Preferred Equities and the federal government. When this did not work out, efforts were directed toward the purchase by the federal government of Preferred Equities' interest in Ash Meadows. U.S. Senator Paul Laxalt from Nevada helped secure an appropriation of federal funds for such a purpose. At his urging, The Nature Conservancy, a national conservation organization, purchased 12,613 acres of land and water rights owned by Preferred Equities in Ash Meadows. The Nature Conservancy paid Preferred Equities $5.5 million plus a $1 million loan at 5 percent interest. In 1984 the U.S. Fish and Wildlife Service purchased the conservancy's Ash Meadows interests for $5 million plus a $500,000 appropriation that came later (Schwartz, 1984:17).

In 1984 the Ash Meadows National Wildlife Refuge was established primarily for conservation of threatened and endangered species found there, to promote all native wildlife, and to provide public recreational opportunities compatible with the primary purpose (A Plan for the Future … , 1988).

Prior to its purchase of the Ash Meadows property from The Nature Conservancy, the U.S. Fish and Wildlife Service prepared an environmental statement on the impact of withdrawal of a large portion of the Ash Meadows area for conservation purposes. The impact statement was particularly interesting from the perspective of Amargosa Valley residents. Supportive of wildlife conservation, they noted that it was not prepared under the standards required by the National Environmental Policy Act and that it devoted considerable discussion to the welfare of the several endangered species in Ash Meadows and to various alternatives for their protection. At the same time, virtually nothing was said concerning the welfare of the human residents of Ash Meadows and the rest of the Amargosa Valley (Jackson, 1987).

Valley residents believed that the preparers of the document, and those behind the land withdrawal, assumed that the welfare of valley residents was irrelevant and undeserving of attention and that from the beginning the effort was based on the assumption that man and the endangered plants and animals of Ash Meadows cannot share the same environment, that human beings must be excluded, except perhaps for a few tourists passing through the area. These assumptions, residents noted, ignored thousands of years of occupation of Ash Meadows by Native Americans and more than 130 years of direct involvement by Europeans and others. Moreover, they contended that Ash Meadows was withdrawn from further development with virtually no input from the residents of the Amargosa Valley—those who would be most affected by the effort—and with no thought to its economic impact, which has been negative. Local residents said they saw the withdrawal as another example of imposition of rule by big government and pressure groups who knew nothing and cared little about the valley's overall welfare. Valley residents pointed out that the endangered species found in Ash Meadows could be preserved in many ways, including the use of designated areas within Ash Meadows.

Atomic Testing at the Nevada Test Site

The testing of nuclear weapons in the South Pacific during the first years following World War II was considered a success; however, security concerns and the necessity of transporting men and equipment thousands of miles from U.S. shores were a constant inconvenience. Nevertheless, Atomic Energy Commission (predecessor of the present U.S. Department of Energy) Commissioner Sumner Pike declared in March 1949 that it would take a national emergency to justify testing within the U.S. borders. Such an emergency arose in 1950 when the Soviet Union detonated its first atomic device and the U.S. became embroiled in the Korean conflict (Titus, 1986:55).

After reviewing five sites in New Mexico, Utah, North Carolina, and northern and southern Nevada, on December 18, 1950, President Truman approved establishment of an atomic testing facility on part of the Las Vegas-Tonopah Bombing and Gunnery Range located in Nye County about 65 miles northwest of Las Vegas. The first detonation of an atomic device on the Test Site took place on January 27, 1951, at Frenchman Flat, located a scant 30 miles from the Amargosa Valley to the northeast over the low-lying Specter Range (Titus, 1986:55-56). Later the facility was expanded; over the next four decades approximately 700 detonations of atomic devices took place, at first in the open atmosphere, then after August 5, 1963, exclusively underground (U.S. DOE, 1989; Titus, 1986:65). Operation of the Nevada Test Site has been, and remains, a major economic stimulus to Nye County and southern Nevada, accounting directly or indirectly for about 9 percent of the workforce in the southern region of the state (Titus, 1986:68). The proximity of the Test Site has led many workers to establish their homes in the Amargosa Valley; the site was an important stimulus for growth in the valley's Farm Area during the 1950s and 1960s (Boyd, 1987; Records, 1987). Perhaps the greatest single influx of Test Site workers and their families into the valley was that associated with the Atomic Energy Commission's efforts to develop a nuclear engine at Jackass Flats during the 1960s.

Originally, the Atomic Energy Commission had planned to build a community, perhaps similar to Los Alamos, New Mexico, in the Amargosa Valley. These plans were abandoned in favor of the Mercury site, however (Records, 1987). Atmospheric tests were easily visible and witnessed by Amargosa Valley residents during the 1950s. Although the testing has given rise to some anxiety among residents through the years, in general the community had a rather accepting view of the nuclear testing program. They recognized potential dangers associated with nuclear testing and understood the possibility of contamination of precious groundwater. Yet they also believed that testing was and remains a necessary activity.

Adjusting to Life in the Amargosa Valley

Betty-Jo Boyd, then Mrs. Tracy W. Smith, and her husband first drove through the Amargosa Valley in about 1960 on their way to a new home in Sacramento, California. Three years later they returned to the valley as residents. In the meantime, Gordon Bettles had passed away and Billie, his wife, had moved out of their home at the T&T Ranch and occupied the house behind the Mecca Inn, located at the junction of the Lathrop Wells-Death Valley Junction highway and Mecca Road. The Smiths bought the Bettles' home on the T&T Ranch (Boyd, 1987).

The new home was spartan—little more than a one-room cabin. Betty-Jo's need for greenery was met by the grass and many trees surrounding the well-watered site on the ranch that had been left by Bettles. All appliances ran on gas, including a stove, refrigerator, and hot-water heater. A small generator provided light for several hours each night. A 60-watt light bulb atop a tall pole on the property was visible at night in Lathrop Wells, miles away (Boyd, 1987).

Betty-Jo remembered that it took time to become accustomed to living in such a remote desert area. Trips to "town," as Las Vegas was known to valley residents, were infrequent—every two weeks at first and then over the years falling off to once a month. People had to learn to buy ahead and plan for meals and other needs weeks in advance. Betty-Jo quickly learned that the desert is a demanding master. In the dry climate and sandy valley soil, plants and trees die rapidly unless they are watered thoroughly and regularly. Betty-Jo emphasized, "Your trees need more attention. Your grass has to be watered often if you're to have any" (Boyd, 1987). Wooden buildings can dry out and deteriorate rapidly and must be constantly maintained to prevent leaking during one of the valley's infrequent rains. Keeping one jump ahead of the dust, which seems to blow into the house through invisible cracks in the walls, is never-ending. As Betty-Jo said, "You're a slave to everything you own out here. It's not a casual way of life. It's a very demanding way of life. You don't live here casually." Even so, she added quickly, "Life in the valley is full" (Boyd, 1987).

By the time the Smiths arrived in the valley in the early 1960s, nuclear testing at the Nevada Test Site was conducted underground. As a new resident in the area, Betty-Jo had no idea what might happen. She found that the shots sometimes produced noticeable ground motion. Lights hanging from cords would swing and the walls of her home would shake; once, a clock was knocked off the wall. Upon arriving, she kept her good dishes on the bed until she had been through several nuclear tests and knew what to expect (Boyd, 1987).

Growth of a Community and Its Government

Many of the newcomers who came to live in the valley during the 1960s were employed at the Test Site, in particular on the nuclear rocket engine program at Jackass Flats. The proximity of Jackass Flats made an easy commute from the valley, especially in comparison to the trip from Las Vegas. A number of individuals filed for land under the Desert Land Act, which was still in force. There was some private effort to develop small lots for those who did not want to go through the Desert Entry process. Residents at the west end of the valley at that time included the Dansbys, the Nickells, the Gareys, Hank and Robert Records, Jill Long, and two Selbach families. As during the 1950s, there were a number of womanless men whose wives remained in a city, where life was more convenient and children were closer to schools. Residents in the Ash Meadows area of the valley included the Rookers, the Tubbs, and Pete Peterson. The two communities were separate socially (Boyd, 1987).

The hub of Amargosa Valley's social life at this time was the post office/restaurant/bar combination at Lathrop Wells. Jane Bonberg was the postmistress, and Harry Pippins ran the bar; Gordon Wagner was the cook in the restaurant. A great deal of time was spent by most community members socializing at the restaurant and bar. Because there was no other place for social interaction, valley residents ate a lot of meals at the restaurant. The bar served as a meeting place for friends and a gathering spot for discussing issues. Additionally, it served as a kind of check station for those temporarily leaving the valley. When individuals went to Las Vegas, for instance, they always stopped at the bar and told the bartender (usually Harry Pippins) that they were leaving. Likewise, they reported in on their return home. Between activities at the post office and the bar, Bonberg and Pippins pretty well knew everybody's business in the valley (Boyd, 1987). Additionally, the Mecca Club, located at the junction of Mecca Road and the Lathrop Wells-Death Valley Junction highway, served as an informal social center, as did the Stateline Saloon after it opened in 1963 (Boyd, 1989).

By about 1964, most valley residents began to recognize the need for a formal community organization. Although the local bars had served their purpose as community gathering places and sites of information exchange, residents began to express the need for a more formal organization, something with legally recognized status. Without it, community members had no way to communicate formally with county or state officials in Tonopah or Carson City. There was also the problem of paying taxes to the county or state without any formal means of making community needs known to officials or any way of bringing the taxes back in the form of development and services. With these problems in mind, valley residents organized the Amargosa Valley Improvement Association, known as AVIA, a nonprofit corporation. William P. Beko, the Nye County district attorney, assisted AVIA in drawing up its charter. Among those associated with the formation of AVIA were the Dansbys, Tommy Nickell, Starr Ellis, and Mike Gilgan (Boyd, 1987). Because AVIA had no church, no school, no government building, and no place beyond the local bars in which to hold meetings, the first order of business became construction of a community building (Boyd, 1987). AVIA obtained a parcel of land and water rights on Farm Road just west of the Lathrop Wells-Death Valley Junction highway, donated by Willard Johns, from Ontario, California; he had obtained the land through the Desert Land Act (Records, 1989). Through volunteer labor provided by residents they constructed a community building, completed in about 1964.

Even during its construction, the AVIA building became a focus of community identity. Functions were even held before the roof was completed. The building was the first tangible evidence that the Amargosa Valley was more than a number of isolated residences and was a viable and growing community of modern pioneers working together on the desert for the common good. Once completed, the AVIA building served as a place for all community meetings and as a center for dances and other social functions, including what became the valley's most important community event—the Amargosa Valley Barbecue that was held each Memorial Day weekend. Records were usually played at the dances, but on special occasions, including Halloween, New Year's Eve, and Memorial Day weekend, live bands were brought in. A variety of children's activities, including 4-H, were also held there (Boyd, 1987).

Thus, AVIA became a sub rosa governing body in the Amargosa Valley. Now the town could formally communicate its needs to the Nye County commissioners. AVIA began sending regular representatives to county commission meetings. In keeping with its role as a community social outlet, AVIA held monthly meetings in conjunction with potluck dinners; these functions became a vital part of valley social life (Boyd, 1987). AVIA had been developed in response to a community need, a pattern repeated as development continued in the future.

There was, for example, a great need for community recreational activities. In its early years AVIA organized and sponsored softball teams, three to five teams each year. A field was graded and maintained near the AVIA building. Amargosa Valley teams played against each other and against teams from Beatty, Furnace Creek, and Indian Springs. Softball was an important AVIA activity for many years, but in the 1980s the interest of many residents began to shift toward car racing. AVIA sponsored car races on its race track constructed near the original AVIA building (Boyd, 1987).

As people continued to move into the valley during the early 1960s, families with small children became more numerous. At first, all children attended school in Beatty. Parents took them to Lathrop Wells, and a county school bus transported them from there to Beatty. Parents were never happy with this arrangement, however, viewing it as especially difficult for the younger children. In the middle 1960s the first attempts to solve the school problem resulted in adapting the AVIA building for use as a schoolhouse. Additionally, a small mobile modular classroom was moved onto the grounds behind the AVIA building. Residents pointed out that at that time the Amargosa Valley was the only community in Nye County that furnished its own building for a school (Boyd, 1987).

Beginning in the 1970s, long-term residents of the Amargosa Valley said, there was an increase in interest in religion and church attendance. Since the 1970s four churches have been established; previously there had been none. These include a Catholic Church, a Mormon Church, and churches representing two Protestant denominations. Some residents saw this as a natural development in the social life of the area. One resident noted,

> It is very interesting to watch [the valley] go from a bar society to a church society. Here we've watched it all, [at first] you never saw anyone unless you went to the bar—but they had food, too, so you didn't necessarily have to drink ...

Then ... [the community] evolved and the [social needs]
were filled by the AVIA, from the AVIA they went to
churches (Boyd, 1987).

Though churches began to be important in the valley, they
by no means replaced the bars as community social centers.
The Stateline Saloon is a case in point. It was built in 1963 by
Slim Thurman and Opie Dyke, located on the Lathrop Wells-
Death Valley Junction highway, just inside the Nevada line.
The men remained partners for a time, then split up, with one
moving to Caliente and becoming associated with another
bar. The other stayed with the Stateline. Fran York, owner of
Fran's Star Ranch brothel, located north of Beatty, bought the
saloon in 1972 for her daughter Michelle Cohan and her son-
in-law Joe. The Cohans ran the bar for eight years and later
brought Doris Jackson in to manage it (Jackson, 1987).

Doris Jackson and her husband first moved to the Amargosa Valley in 1973 and purchased 60 acres in the northwest
area. There they grew fruit and nut trees, including almonds,
figs, nectarines, apples, cherries, peaches, and apricots. They
also raised grapes, including Zinfandels, California Red,
Thompson Seedless, and Concords. They grew alfalfa by
irrigating it with wheel lines, and they kept goats and chickens, selling goat's milk and eggs. Life on a farm in the Amargosa Valley was a marked contrast to the glamour Doris Jackson had experienced working at Caesars Palace, where she
was employed prior to moving to the valley (Jackson, 1987).

Jackson's experience in the Las Vegas casinos and her
understanding of local residents formed a felicitous combination. In the first two months she managed the Stateline Saloon
she tripled the gross receipts. Dances, a happy hour, and such
events as wet T-shirt contests all went over well. Her secret
was that she treated people as she would want to be treated.

Sufficiently satisfied with her managerial skills, she took an option on the Stateline and applied for a gaming license. In 1982 she was approved by the Nevada Gaming Commission, and became the state's first female holder of a gaming license for an establishment wholly owned by a woman. After receiving the license, Jackson purchased the saloon and soon began expanding the facility (Jackson, 1987).

Under Jackson's ownership, the Stateline Saloon has become more than just a saloon. It is often a focus of community organization, second only to town government and the churches. Holidays—such as Valentine's Day, Easter, Fourth of July, Thanksgiving, and Christmas—are celebrated with dinner and a dance and singing at the Stateline. Birthday parties for senior citizens include live music, dinner, and prizes for winners of contests held during the event. On Easter Sunday, the saloon sponsors an Easter egg hunt for children in the valley; the tots have first crack at trying to find the less well-hidden eggs, and the older kids are challenged to find the eggs that are more cleverly concealed. The Stateline serves food as well as drink; everyone is welcome even just to talk. Moreover, the establishment has an additional extra special attraction—one of the most beautiful and picturesque desert views that a resident or traveler could ever hope to see—a stunning panorama of the south end of the Funeral Mountains, which when viewed through the saloon's front picture window looks as though John Ford, the cinematic chronicler of the pioneer West, had personally framed it.

The Mecca Club, for which Mecca Road was later named, located at the junction of Mecca Road and the Lathrop Wells-Death Valley Junction highway, was constructed about 1959 by Gordon and Billie Bettles, with funding provided by the owner of the Moulin Rouge in Las Vegas. In the years following Gordon Bettles' death, it went through a series of owners, including Hank Records, who had it in 1969-1970 (Records, 1989). It was later purchased by Sherry and Gene Richey, who turned it into a brothel and changed its name to the Crystal Palace. When the couple divorced, the brothel folded. This pleased many community members, who had never liked the idea of a brothel in the center of the valley. A bar named the Amargosa Club later opened at the site (Jackson, 1987).

Amargosa Becomes an Unincorporated Town

The increased population in the valley produced by the American Borate Company and IMV operations in the 1970s brought more residents and a resultant increased demand for community services. The larger population and tax base led increasingly to the realization that the old AVIA organization was not effective enough in communicating community needs to county government. Consequently, residents began circulating petitions asking for designation of the Amargosa Valley as an unincorporated town. A large percentage of valley residents signed these petitions, and they were presented to the Nye County commissioners. Amargosa Valley was given formal designation as an unincorporated town, and its boundaries were drawn in 1982. The town covers most of the Amargosa Valley and is the second largest such community in the United States, encompassing 480 square miles (Boyd, 1987; Jackson, 1987).

Following the status change, members of the Amargosa Valley Town Advisory Council were summarily elected. The board holds monthly meetings in the valley and also meets on the first Tuesday of each month with the Nye County commissioners. Members are elected by popular vote; three serve for three years and two for two years. All issues are put to a vote at council meetings. And the system works. As Doris Jackson, a present Advisory Council member, noted, "Even though sometimes things get voted down I personally would like, maybe later down the road, I see why it got voted down. It is like going back to the village square and having open meetings, which our democracy is built on" (Jackson, 1987).

Roads have been an important priority for the council, and work is progressing on a community park and cemetery. (In years past, many valley residents were buried in Beatty.) Demands for increased community facilities and services led to the recognition that the old AVIA building and adjoining facilities had been outgrown. "Being good true Americans," Doris Jackson jokingly said, "the first thing we [the Advisory Council] did was run in debt" (Jackson, 1987). An election was held to float bonds for the construction of a new community center, a clinic, and a library. Construction of all three was completed in 1984. Though the ABC mining operation closed and there were fewer people living in the valley, the community buildings, completed in the middle 1980s, serve as the focal point of community pride and identity, despite the fact that the reduced population in the valley and the debt they have assumed means that Amargosa residents have the highest taxes in Nye County (Jackson, 1987).

CHAPTER 9

The Future

margosa Valley residents are unanimous in their love for their valley and the life-style they lead. And despite economic setbacks in the 1970s and 1980s (cessation of farming at Ash Meadows and fluctuations in mining and employment at the Nevada Test Site), valley residents look to the future with optimism. They know the valley's resources, the quality of life the valley offers, and the unparalleled opportunities to experience the beauty and enjoy the solitude and freedom of the desert. They are convinced the Amargosa Valley will continue to be a place in which residents can earn a good living or retire. Growth is encouraged by valley residents as long as it is not excessive.

Valley residents are confident that they will prevail in controversies over wild horses and development of the valley's water resources. They are pleased that ABC has reopened (though on a limited basis) and enthusiastically support Nye County's effort to locate a modern science museum near the intersection of U.S. Highway 95 and State Highway 373. Residents believe the development and promotion of the Ash

Meadows National Wildlife Refuge, the proposed science museum, and the valley's proximity to Death Valley will bring more tourists to the area.

Many people believe that their community will continue to play an important role in research and development in both defense and nondefense industries. They are proud of their pioneering role in the development of nuclear weapons and in research on such projects as the nuclear rocket engine.

Residents of the Amargosa Valley may once again be front-row observers, and possibly participants, in a major federal nuclear program: the disposal of the nation's spent fuel and high-level radioactive waste in a manner that protects the health and safety of the public. In 1987 the U.S. Congress selected Yucca Mountain, located in the northern part of the valley, as the preferred site for the nation's first underground, high-level nuclear waste repository. A repository may be constructed inside Yucca Mountain if the site is proven to be geotechnically suitable. Although the suitability of the site may not be known until the beginning of the next century, many residents view the location of a nuclear waste repository at Yucca Mountain as a challenge because the safe disposal of nuclear waste would benefit humanity and the environment. They believe that negative impacts of a repository must be avoided and positive effects maximized. They view with dismay the words and efforts of those who would abandon nuclear technology because of its difficulties. The new pioneers in the Amargosa Valley believe that nuclear technology and the desert, with its freedom and incredible beauty, can coexist productively and harmoniously.

References

"A Plan for the Future Ash Meadows National Wildlife Refuge." U.S. Department of Interior, U.S. Fish and Wildlife Service. RF 14554. 1988.

Belden, L. Burr. "Dad Fairbanks Founded Towns, Rescued Scores." *San Bernardino Sun-Telegram*, p. 34. December 5, 1954.

———. *Goodbye Death Valley*. Bishop, CA: Chalfant Press, Inc. 1956.

Blair, Lynda. Personal communication. 1989.

Boyd, Betty-Jo Smith. *An Interview with Betty-Jo Smith Boyd*. Nye County Town History Project, Tonopah, NV. 1987.

———. Personal communication. 1989.

Bradhurst, Stephen T. Personal communication. 1987.

Brennan, Irene J. "'Diamond-tooth' Lil." *Las Vegas Review-Journal*, "Nevadan," pp. 30-31. February 23, 1975.

Brockman, Frank and Edith. *An Interview with Frank and Edith Brockman*. Nye County Town History Project, Tonopah, NV. 1987.

Brooks, Richard H., and Daniel Larson. *Preliminary Archaeological*

Field Reconnaissance in the Amargosa Basin. Nevada Archaeological Survey. 1973.

Brooks, Thomas W. Edited, with introductory notes by Anthony L. Lehman. *By Buckboard to Beatty: The California-Nevada Desert in 1886.* Los Angeles: Dawson's Book Shop. 1970.

Carlson, Helen S. *Nevada Place Names: A Geographical Dictionary.* Reno: University of Nevada Press. 1974.

"Carrara Founder Dies in Kentucky." *Beatty Bulletin.* June 3, 1955.

Cline, Gloria Griffen. *Peter Skene Ogden and the Hudson's Bay Company.* Norman: University of Oklahoma Press. 1974.

Colvin, James H. "Sam." *An Interview with James H. "Sam" Colvin.* Nye County Town History Project, Tonopah, NV. 1987

Cook, Sid F., and Cynthia D. Williams. *The Status and Future of Ash Meadows, Nye County, Nevada.* Carson City: Office of the Attorney General, State of Nevada. 1982.

D'Azevedo, Warren L., ed. *Great Basin.* Handbook of North American Indians, Vol. 11. Washington, DC: Smithsonian Institution. 1986.

Doherty, John. "The History of the Settling of the Manse Ranch and Territory." *Nevada Historical Society Quarterly,* pp. 165-168. Fall 1974.

Dymond, Tom. Personal communication. 1989.

Egan, Ferol. *Fremont: Explorer for a Restless Nation.* Reno: University of Nevada Press. 1985.

Fishel, Robert J. Personal communication. 1990.

Gower, Harry P. *50 Years in Death Valley—Memoirs of a Borax Man.* Introduction by James M. Gerstley. Published by the Death Valley '49ers. Publication No. 9. San Bernardino, CA: Inland Printing and Engraving Company. 1969.

Hansen, Ernest H. "Forrest." *An Interview with Ernest H. "Forrest" Hansen.* Nye County Town History Project, Tonopah, NV. 1987.

Industrial Mineral Ventures, Inc. "Proposed clay mining and processing in the Amargosa Desert, Nevada, California." Golden, CO: Industrial Mineral Ventures, Inc. 1973.

Jackson, Doris M. *An Interview with Doris M. Jackson.* Nye County Town History Project, Tonopah, NV. 1987.

————. Personal communication. 1989.

James, Susan. "Blazing a Trail with Blasdel." *Nevada Magazine.* September/October. P. 19. 1989.

Johnson, Leroy and Jean. *Escape from Death Valley.* Reno: University of Nevada Press. 1987.

Lee, Bourke. *Death Valley.* New York: Macmillan Co. 1930.

Lewis, Georgia. "Jack Longstreet—Southern Nevada gunslinger who lived to be 93 years old." *Las Vegas Review-Journal,* "Nevadan," pp. 3-5. May 18, 1969.

Lingenfelter, Richard E. *Death Valley and the Amargosa: A Land of Illusion.* Berkeley: University of California Press. 1986.

Lisle, Betty. "Dad Fairbanks, Desert Pioneer." *Las Vegas Review-Journal,* "Nevadan," pp. 4-5. January 13, 1974(a).

————. "Mother Opened the Whiskey Barrel Spigot." *Las Vegas Review-Journal,* "Nevadan," p. 4. January 20, 1974(b).

Lisle, Ralph F. Personal communication. 1989.

Lowe, Celesta Lisle. *An Interview with Celesta Lowe.* Nye County Town History Project, Tonopah, NV. 1988.

Lowe, Deke. *An Interview with Deke Lowe.* Nye County Town History Project, Tonopah, NV. 1988.

————. Personal communication. 1989.

Lyle, D. A. "The Springs of Southern Nevada." *American Naturalist.* Vol. 21, pp. 18-27. 1878.

McCracken, Robert D. *History Reports and Literature Reviews: Clark County, Henderson, Indian Springs, Las Vegas, and North Las Vegas,*

Nevada; History Reports and Literature Reviews: Nye County, Amargosa Valley, Beatty, and Pahrump, Nevada. Vols. 1 and 2. SAIC, 101 Convention Center Drive, Las Vegas, NV 89109. 1986.

Morgan, Dale L. *Jedediah Smith and the Opening of the West.* Indianapolis, IN: Bobbs Merrill Co. 1953.

Myrick, David F. *Railroads of Nevada and Eastern California.* Berkeley: Howell-North Books. 2 vols. 1962, 1963.

Nevada Department of Conservation and Natural Resources. Untitled paper provided by Rick Robinson. 5 pp. 1985.

Noren, Evelyn. "John Fremont Dared What Others Dreamed." *Las Vegas Review-Journal,* "Nevadan," pp. 6L-7L. December 12, 1982.

Palmer, T. S., ed. *Place Names of the Death Valley Region in California and Nevada.* Morongo Valley, CA: Sagebrush Press. 1980.

Potts, Donald B. Personal communication. 1989.

Rafferty, Kevin. Personal communication. 1989.

Records, Henry A. "Hank." *An Interview with Henry A. "Hank" Records.* Nye County Town History Project, Tonopah, NV. 1987.

———. Personal communication. 1989.

———. Personal communication. 1990.

Reeder, Ray M. "The Mormon Trail, A History of the Salt Lake to Los Angeles Route to 1869." Unpublished Ph.D. dissertation. Provo, UT: Brigham Young University. May 1966.

Reidhead, Boyd and Claudia. Personal communication. 1987.

Revert, Robert A. *An Interview with Robert A. Revert.* Nye County Town History Project, Tonopah, NV. 1988.

Rooker, Norine. *An Interview with Norine Rooker.* Nye County Town History Project, Tonopah, NV. 1987.

Roske, Ralph J. Personal communication. 1986.

Sada, Donald W. *Proposed Acquisition to Establish Ash Meadows Na-*

tional Wildlife Refuge, Nye County, Nevada. Portland, OR: Department of the Interior, U.S. Fish and Wildlife Service. 1984.

Schwartz, Anne. "Bright Future for a Desert Refugium." *The Nature Conservancy News*. Vol. 34, No. 5, pp. 13-17. September/October 1984.

Slavin, Edward R. Personal communication. 1989.

Spears, John R. *Illustrated Sketches of Death Valley and Other Borax Deserts of the Pacific Coast*. Chicago and New York: Rand, McNally & Co., 1892. Reissued by Sagebrush Press, Morongo Valley, CA, 1977.

Squires, Charles P. and Delphine A. "Las Vegas, Nevada: Its Romance and History." Manuscript. Las Vegas, NV. 1955.

The Statutes at Large of the United States of America from May, 1919, to March, 1921. Vol. XLI. Part 1. Washington, DC: U.S. Government Printing Office. 1921.

Sternberg, Sherry. Untitled manuscript on the history of the Valley Electric Association, Inc., later published in segments in *Ruralite* (Ruralite Services, Inc., Forest Grove, OR). 1986.

Steward, Julian H. *Basin-Plateau Aboriginal Sociopolitical Groups*. Washington, DC: Bureau of American Ethnology Bulletin 120. 1938. Reprinted by University of Utah Press, Salt Lake City. 1970.

"Sticht Wins Decision in Ash Meadows Suit." *Beatty Bulletin*. August 11, 1950.

Stretch, R. H. "Journal of Explorations in Southern Nevada in the Spring of 1866" in Report of the State Mineralogist of Nevada. Journal of the Senate during the Third Session ... 1867. "Appendix E." Pp. 141-147.

Thybony, Scott. "Man, Fish Find Danger Under Desert Floor." *Los Angeles Times*, Pp. 3. May 3, 1987.

Titus, A. Costandina. *Bombs in the Backyard*. Reno: University of Nevada Press. 1986.

Toles, Herbert L. *An Interview with Herbert L. Toles*. Nye County Town History Project, Tonopah, NV. 1987.

————. Personal communication. 1990.

Trexler, Dennis T., and Wilton N. Melhorn. "Singing and Booming Sand Dunes of California and Nevada." *California Geology.* July. Pp. 147-152. 1986.

U.S. Department of Energy. Nevada Office. Personal communication. July 17, 1989.

Warren, Elizabeth von Till. "Armijo's Trace Revisited: A New Interpretation of the Impact of the Antonio Armijo Route of 1829-30 on the Development of the Old Spanish Trail." Unpublished M.A. thesis. Las Vegas: University of Nevada. 1974.

————. "History of the Amargosa-Mojave Planning Units" in Claude N. Warren, Martha Knack, and Elizabeth von Till Warren. *A Cultural Resource Overview for the Amargosa Mojave Basin Planning Units*, pp. 195-257. Las Vegas: University of Nevada. 1980.

Wheat, Carl I. "Pioneer Visitors to Death Valley After the Forty-Niners." *Quarterly* (California Historical Society), Vol. 18, No. 3. Pp. 1-22. 1939.

Wheeler, George M. *Preliminary Report Concerning Explorations and Surveys Principally in Nevada and Arizona.* Washington, DC: U.S. Government Printing Office. Appendix B report by D. A. Lyle. 1871.

Zanjani, Sally. "Jack Longstreet in the Death Valley Region." Paper given at the Death Valley Conference on Death Valley History, Furnace Creek, CA. February 8, 1987.

————. *Jack Longstreet: Last of the Desert Frontiersmen.* Athens, OH: Swallow/Ohio University Press. 1988.

Index

ABC. *See* American Borate
   Company
Agriculture, in Amargosa Valley/
   Ash Meadows, 67, 69, 77, 78,
   79-80, 83, 93, 105
   in 1800s, 27, 29
   markets for, 82-83
Alfalfa, 79, 80, 105
   on Spring Meadows Ranch, 94
   See also Agriculture
Amargosa, meaning of (Spanish), 2
Amargosa Club, 107
Amargosa Desert, 1, 2, 13, 20, 25,
   26. *See also* Amargosa Valley
Amargosa Hotel, 69
Amargosa Mountains. *See* Funeral
   Mountains
Amargosa River, 2, 5, 16, 20, 29
Amargosa Valley
   agriculture in. *See* Agriculture
   climate, 1, 2, 23-24, 81, 100
   early exploration, 9-17, 19-26
   economic development, 47, 75,
      82-83, 92, 97, 98-99, 107, 109-
      110

electricity. *See* Electricity, in
   Amargosa Valley
Farm Area, 80, 99
geography/topography, 1-4, 10,
   14-15. *See also* Big Dune
prehistory of, 4-8
unincorporated town, 73, 107-
   108
Amargosa Valley Barbecue
   (Memorial Day), 103. *See also*
   AVIA
Amargosa Valley Electric Coop-
   erative, 85, 86. *See also*
   Electricity, in Amargosa
   Valley
Amargosa Valley Improvement
   Association. *See* AVIA
Amargosa Valley Town Advisory
   Council, 107-108. *See also*
   Amargosa Valley, unincorpo-
   rated town
American Borate Company (ABC),
   92, 107, 108, 109
American Carrara Marble Com-
   pany, 73, 74. *See also* Carrara,

marble quarry; Perkins, P. V.
Anasazi indians. *See under* Indians
Annabella (UT)
Dad Fairbanks and, 49-50, 51
Arcan, John, 17-18. *See also*
Bennett-Arcan wagon party
Armijo, Antonio, 9
Ash Meadows, 2-3, 5, 13, 14-15, 24,
27, 31, 75, 109
cattle ranching in, 27, 28, 94
early descriptions of, 14-16, 25-
26, 33-34
endemic species, 94
1930s-1950s, 70-74, 101
outlaw territory, 56, 87, 88
during Prohibition, 56-58
railroad stop at, 45. *See also*
Fairbanks Spring Ranch
Ash Meadows Lodge, 72
Ash Meadows National Wildlife
Refuge, 96, 109. *See also* En-
dangered species; Environ-
mental movement
Ash Meadows Valley, 5
clay deposits, 58-59, 60-63, 71, 88
Associated Oil Company
Dad Fairbanks and, 54
Associated Pit (clay deposit), 71
Atomic Energy Commission, 98,
99
Atomic weapons testing, 98-99,
110. *See also* Nevada Test Site
Audubon Society, 96. *See also*
Environmental movement
AVIA (Amargosa Valley Improve-
ment Association), 102-104,
105, 108

Baker (CA)
Dad Fairbanks and, 54-55
Bars, 101, 102, 104, 105-107. *See also*
Amargosa Club; Mecca Club;
Stateline Saloon
Beatty (NV), 43, 44, 86
early Indian population, 7

ranches near, 29
schools, 104
Beaver Dam Wash, 13
Beko, William P., 102
Bell Pit (clay deposit), 71
Bennett, Asabell (family), 12. *See
also* Bennett-Arcan wagon
party
Bennett, Charles, 39
Bennett-Arcan wagon party, 13-14,
15, 16-17
Bentonite clay. *See under* Clay
Bettles, Billie (Willie Odetta
McElrath), 76, 77-78, 87
and Mecca Club, 106
and T&T Ranch, 69, 75, 77, 99
Bettles, Gordon, 75-76, 77-78, 99
and Mecca Club, 106
and T&T Ranch, 69-70, 75, 77
Big Dune, 3-4, 5
Big Spring, 36
Billy Mine (borax), 91
Birch Creek, 18
Black, Fannie, 31
Blasdel, Henry Goode, 21, 22
Bloody Gulch (NV), 57
Boggs, G. Ray, 59
Bole's Spring, 36
Bonberg, Jane, 101, 102
Bonner Springs, 22
Borate (Calico) (CA), 42
Borax, 41-42, 91
processing, in Amargosa Valley,
91
prospecting, 38-39
workers, 92
See also American Borate
Company; Lila C. Mine;
Smith, F. M.
Boulder Dam. *See* Hoover Dam.
See also Electricity, in Amar-
gosa Valley
Bowman, Elmer, 85
Boyd, Betty-Jo, 99, 100
and T&T Ranch, 99-101

Bradford homestead, 72
Bradford Mill, 71
Bradford Siding, 58, 59, 65, 71
Breyfogle, Charles C., 18-19, 21. *See also* Lost Breyfogle Lode
"Breyfogling," 19
Brier, Rev. James (family), 12, 13, 16. *See also* Smith, Orson K., wagon party
Brock, Frank S., 58
Brockman, Edith, 76-77, 78
Brockman, Frank, 76-77
Brooks, T. W., 33-36
Brothels, in Amargosa Valley, 58, 72, 79, 107. *See also* Crystal Palace
Brown, Charles A., 53
Bugsmashers, 12, 13, 16. *See also* Smith, Orson K., wagon party
Bullfrog (NV)
ore discoveries, 42
Bullfrog Goldfield Railroad, 44, 45
Bullfrog mining district, 41
Bureau of Land Management, 93
Burros
near Ash Meadows (1920s), 57

Cahill, W. W., 68
Calico (CA). *See* Borate
California Gold Rush (1849), 10-11, 12, 18. *See also* Bennett-Arcan wagon party; Hunt, Jefferson, wagon party, Smith, Orson K., wagon party
Car racing, 104. *See also* AVIA
Carrara (NV), 45, 66, 73-74
marble quarry, 73
mill, 74
Carson City (NV), 21
Carson Slough, 3, 14
peat mining, 93
Cattle ranching,
in Ash Meadows, 28, 34-35, 62, 94
Cedar City (UT), 12

Charleston Peak, 5
Chespa Mine, 31
Chief Tecopa (S. Paiute), 7
Chloride Cliff, 20, 28
Churches, 104-105. *See also* Religion
Clark, William A. (Sen.)
Las Vegas and Tonopah Railroad, 42
San Pedro, Los Angeles, and Salt Lake Railroad, 41, 42
Clay
in Ash Meadows, 58-63, 71, 88. *See also* Ash Meadows Valley, clay deposits
bentonite, 88, 90
hectorite, 90
processing of, 59-60, 89, 90
sepiolite, 89-90
smectite, 90
See also Clay Camp; Industrial Mineral Ventures, Inc.; Vanderbilt Mine
Clay Camp, 61-63, 71
Cohan, Joe, 105
Cohan, Michelle, 105
Cohen, George W., 60
Cohen Companies, 60, 71
Coleman, William T., 39, 91. *See also* Harmony Borax Works
Colemanite. *See* Borax
Collins Spring, 13
Colorado River, 9, 19, 24
dams, 86
Community organizations and activities, 102, 103-104, 108. *See also* Amargosa Valley Barbecue; AVIA; Entertainment
Cox Creek, 16
Crucero (CA), 45, 46
Crystal Palace (brothel), 107
Crystal Springs (NV), 22, 57, 62

Dalton, Ralph, 85

Dansby family, 101, 102
Davies, Fred, 56
Davis Dam, 86. *See also* Electricity, in Amargosa Valley
Death Valley, 10, 13, 16, 17-18, 21-22, 110
    borax discoveries, 38, 42
    mining operations, 26, 91
    See also California Gold Rush
Death Valley Junction, 13, 14, 15, 20, 45, 70
    clay mill, 59-60, 70-71
    electricity in, 85, 87
    population (1931), 70
Death Valley National Monument, 91, 95
Desert Land Act, 70, 75, 78, 79, 101, 103
Devils Hole, 13, 14, 15
    part of Death Valley National Monument, 95
    pupfish controversy, 94, 95
    water levels, 95
Diamondfield Jack
    at Fairbanks Spring Ranch, 53
Diamond-tooth Lil
    at Fairbanks Spring Ranch, 53
Doheny, Edward L., 61
Dyke, Opie, 105

Eagle Mountain (Amargosa Butte), 20
Eastabrooks, Gene, 85
Education. *See* Schools
Electricity
    in Amargosa Valley, 81, 84-87
    in Death Valley Junction, 85, 87
    on T&T Ranch (1960s), 100
Elizalde family, 73
Ellis, Starr, 102
Endangered species
    in Ash Meadows area, 94, 95, 96. *See also* Devils Hole, pupfish controversy; *under* Environmental movement

Enterprise (UT), 12
Entertainment
    in Amargosa Valley, 103, 105-106. *See also* AVIA
    at Clay Camp (1930s), 71-72
    at Lathrop Wells (1950s), 101-102
Environmental movement
    against subdivision of land in Ash Meadows, 96
    defense of endangered species, 95, 96. *See also* Devils Hole, pupfish controversy
    impact statement, 97
Exploration. *See* Amargosa Valley, early exploration

Fairbanks, Celesta, 51, 52, 60
Fairbanks, Celestia, 49, 51-52, 55
Fairbanks, Ralph Jacobus "Dad," 47, 48-51, 53, 54-56. *See also* Fairbanks Mercantile; Fairbanks Spring Ranch
Fairbanks, Stella, 53
Fairbanks, Vonola, 55
Fairbanks family, 47-48, 51, 55
Fairbanks Mercantile, 50, 51, 53
Fairbanks Spring, 25, 36
Fairbanks Spring Ranch, 36, 50, 51, 52-53. *See also* Fairbanks, Ralph Jacobus "Dad"
Farm Area. *See under* Amargosa Valley
Farm Road, 102
Fishel, Robert J., 69
Fish Lake Valley, 24, 87
Forman, Charles, 28
Forman, Grant. *See* Forman, Charles
Fortymile Canyon, 16
Forty-niners. *See* California Gold Rush
Fox, L. T., 28
Fran's Star Ranch (brothel), 105
Fremont, John C.

1844 expedition, 10
1845-1846 expedition, 10
1853 expedition, 19
French, E. Darwin (Dr.), 19
Frenchman Flat
  atomic weapons testing, 98. *See also* Nevada Test Site
Fuller's earth, 60. *See also* Clay
Funeral Mountains (Amargosa Mountains), 5, 13, 20, 21, 22, 25, 106
  mountain sheep in, 6
Furnace Creek, 19, 22, 24, 85, 87
Furnace Creek Inn, 13, 69
Furnace Creek Wash, 13, 15, 16, 21, 22, 70
  borax mine near, 91

Gallopin' Goose, 70
Garey family, 101
General Petroleum (subsidiary of Standard Oil)
  Ash Meadows clay deposits, 58
Geneva (NV), 18
Gilgan, Mike, 102
Glessner, M. P. "Gles," 77
Glessner, Pat, 77
Gold Center (NV), 66-67, 73
  railroads at, 43, 44
Goldfield (NV), 42
Gower, Harry P., 67-68, 70, 76
  manager of T&T Ranch, 67-68, 75
Great Basin, 25
  mapping of, 10, 11, 12
Greenwater (CA), 52
  Fairbanks freighting business, 50, 51, 53

Harmony Borax Works, 39
Hawes Canyon, 31
Henderson, Lee
  and Mizpah Garage, 32
Highway 95, 13, 80, 109
Highway 129. *See* Lathrop

Wells–Death Valley Junction highway
Highway 190, 13
Highway 373, 109. *See also* Lathrop Wells–Death Valley Junction highway
Hiko (NV), 22
Homestead Act, 68, 79
Homesteads, in Amargosa Valley, 29, 31
Hoover Dam, 86
Horses, wild, 109
Horse thieves, 10
Houghton, J. F., 19
Hunt, Jefferson
  wagon party, 11, 12, 16
Hunting, 6. *See also* Indians, hunting and gathering

Illustrated Sketches of Death Valley (Spears), 37-38
IMV. *See* Industrial Mineral Ventures, Inc.
Indians, in Amargosa Valley
  Anasazi, 4
  fall festivals, 6, 8
  hunting and gathering, 4, 5, 6, 7-8
  relations with whites, 26, 56
  Southern Paiute, 4-7, 19, 34
  Ute, 10, 11. *See also* Walkara
  Western Shoshone, 4, 5, 7-8
Indian Springs, 24, 26, 42
Industrial Mineral Ventures, Inc. (IMV), 89-91, 95, 107
Interstate Highway 15, 12
Ishmael George, 58-59
Ivanpah (CA), 28, 29
Ives, Butler, 19

Jackass Flats, 101
Jack Longstreet: Last of the Desert Frontiersmen (Zanjani), 30
Jackson, Doris
  and Advisory Council, 107-108

and Stateline Saloon, 92-93, 105-106
Jap Ranch, 72
Jayhawkers, 12, 13, 16, 17. *See also* Smith, Orson K., wagon party
Jenifer, F. M. , 68
Jepperson, Glen, 72
Johnnie Mine, 26
Johnnie Siding (NV), 51
Johns, Willard, 102-103

Kawich Mountains, 31
Keeler, Fred E., 60
Kidder, J. F., 19
Kimball Brothers stage, 51
King, Charles, 27-28, 37

Lancaster (CA), 82
Las Vegas (NV), 41, 42, 56, 82, 84, 86, 100, 101-102
railroads, 42, 43, 50, 51
Las Vegas and Tonopah Railroad (LV&T), 42-43, 50, 51, 73. *See also* Clark, William A.
Las Vegas–Tonopah Bombing and Gunnery Range
atomic testing facility, 98
Las Vegas Valley, 86
Lathrop Wells (NV), 16, 72–73, 75, 79
electricity in, 87
post office/restaurant/bar, 101
Lathrop Wells–Death Valley Junction highway, 69, 78, 92, 102, 105, 106
Law enforcement, in Amargosa Valley/Ash Meadows, 56, 87-88
Lawson, James, 19
Laxalt, Paul (U.S. Sen.), 96
Lear, William
runway at Lathrop Wells, 73
Lee, Leander (Cub), 28-29
borax discovery, 39
Lee, Philander (Phi), 28-29

borax discovery, 39
Leeland (NV), 66
Leeland Station, 67
Leeland Water & Land Company, 69
Lehman, Anthony L., 35-36
Lila C. Mine (borax), 39, 42, 43, 45. *See also* Smith, F. M.
Lisle, John Quincy (Jack), 52, 57, 60, 61
Lisle, Ralph, 57-58
Long, Jill, 101
Longstreet, Andrew Jackson (Jack), 30-32, 56
ranch at Hawes Canyon, 31
Los Angeles (CA), 82
railroad to, 44-45
Lost Breyfogle Lode (gold), 19, 30
Lost Gunsight Lode (silver-lead), 18, 19
Lost Wagons (NV), 16, 21
Lowe, Celesta Lisle, 61, 88
and Dad Fairbanks, 55
Lowe, Deke, 36
Ludlow (CA)
and T&T Railroad, 43, 44, 45, 46
LV&T. *See* Las Vegas and Tonopah Railroad
Lyle, D.A., 24-26

Mankinen, Ed, 85
Mankinen family, 80
Manly, William L., 13, 14, 16, 17
early description of Ash Meadows, 14-15
Manse Ranch, 26, 36
Marble. *See* Carrara
Martin, Jim, 18
Masonic Lodge
Gordon Bettles and, 78
Mayfield, Walter, 67
Mecca Club, 102, 106. *See also* Crystal Palace
Mecca Inn, 99
Mecca Road, 102, 106

Miller, U.S., 68
Mina (NV), 76
Mojave Desert, 46
Monte Blanco borax deposit, 39
Montgomery City (NV), 21
Moonshine. *See* Prohibition
Moreland, Wes, 58
Mormon Church, 49-50, 104
Mormons
  prospecting expeditions in
    Amargosa Valley, 19
  settlements in Salt Lake Valley,
    10, 11
  settlements in southern Utah,
    49, 50
Mormon Trail, 9, 16
Mount Misery (chasm), 13, 17, 18
Mount Sterling, 16

National Rural Electric Cooperative Association, 86. *See also*
  Amargosa Valley Electric
  Cooperative
National Wildlife Federation, 96.
  See also Environmental
  movement
Nature Conservatory, The
  (conservation organization),
  96. *See also* Environmental
  movement
Nevada Department of Highways,
  43
  station at Lathrop Wells, 72
Nevada Gaming Commission,
  106
Nevada Power Company, 84, 85,
  86. *See also* Electricity, in
  Amargosa Valley
Nevada Test Site, 72, 80, 85, 98-99,
  100, 101, 109
  nuclear rocket engine program,
  101, 110
Nickell, Tommy, 102
Nickell family, 101
Nuclear waste repository (Yucca
Mountain), 110
Nuclear weapons testing. *See*
  Atomic weapons testing
Nusbaumer, Louis
  early description of Ash
    Meadows, 15-16. *See also*
    Bennett-Arcan wagon party
Nye County, 87, 88
  commissioners, 107
  economy, 98
  taxes, 108

Oasis Valley, 30, 33
Ogden, Peter Skene
  expedition (1829-1930), 9-10
Old Spanish Trail, 9, 10, 11, 16, 20
Orkhill, F. W., 68
Osgood Mountains, 93
Overland Hotel (Las Vegas), 51
Owen, J.R.N. (Dr.)
  1861 expedition, 19, 20
Owens Lake, 20
Owens Valley, 38

Pacific Coast Borax Company, 59,
  67, 68, 69, 70
  in Death Valley Junction, 70
  See also T&T Ranch; *under* Smith,
    F. M.
Pahranagat mining district, 21, 22
Pahrump (NV), 85, 86
Pahrump Ranch, 39
Pahrump Valley, 9, 10, 26, 29, 33,
  43
Pahrump Valley Utility Company,
  85
Paiute indians. *See* Indians,
  Southern Paiute
Palmer, T. S. (*Place Names of the
  Death Valley Region in Califor-
  nia and Nevada*), 1
Panamint Mountains, 17, 26, 28
Panamint Valley, 20
Papoose Dry Lake, 13
Pardee, Jack, 72

Payson (UT)
    Dad Fairbanks and, 48-49
Peat mining. *See under* Carson
    Slough
Perkins, P. V., 74. *See also* Ameri-
    can Carrara Marble Company
Peterson, Pete, 79, 101
Petting, Harry
    service station, 79
Pike, Sumner, 98
Pine nuts
    Paiute gathering of, 5
    Shoshone harvesting of, 7-8
Pippins, Harry, 101, 102
*Place Names of the Death Valley
    Region in California and Nevada*
    (Palmer), 1
Plumb, C. M.
    description of Winters' home,
    37-38
Point of Rocks gap, 42
Point of Rocks Spring, 28
Post office
    at Lathrop Wells, 101
Potosi Mines, 20
Preferred Equities, 95-96
    purchase of Spring Meadows
    Ranch, 95
Prescott, Edward P., 88. *See also*
    Industrial Mineral Ventures,
    Inc.
Prescott, W. Howard, Jr., 88. *See
    also* Industrial Mineral
    Ventures, Inc.
Prohibition
    stills in Ash Meadows region,
    56-57, 88
Providence Mountains, 20
Pupfish
    Ash Meadows subspecies, 94
    controversy over, in Ash
    Meadows, 94-95
    Devils Hole subspecies, 94
    Warm Springs subspecies,
    94

    See also Devils Hole, pupfish
        controversy; Endangered
        species; Environmental
        movement

Railroads
    in Amargosa Valley, 41-46, 70
    for clay processing, 59, 71
    See also individual railroads
Records, H. H. "Hank," 78-80, 81,
    83, 101
    electric cooperative, 84-85, 86.
    See also Amargosa Valley
    Electric Cooperative
    and Mecca Club, 107
    and T&T Ranch, 70, 80
Records, Robert, 78-80, 83, 101
    electric cooperative, 84-85. *See
    also* Amargosa Valley Electric
    Cooperative
Religion, in Amargosa Valley, 104.
    See also Churches; Mormon
    Church
Resting Spring, 16, 20
Revert, Robert, 88
Rhyolite (NV)
    railroad stop, 43
Richey, Gene, 107
Richey, Sherry, 107
Roads, 80-81, 108. *See also individ-
    ual roads and highways*
Rogers, John H., 13, 17
Rooker family, 101
Rural Electric Administration, 85.
    See also Amargosa Valley
    Electric Cooperative

St. Joseph (NV)
    Dad Fairbanks and, 48
San Antonio Mountains, 24
Sand dunes, singing, 3. *See also* Big
    Dune
Sand Mountain dune, 3
San Pedro, Los Angeles, and Salt
    Lake Railroad (SP, LA&SL),

41, 42, 50, 65. *See also* Clark, William A.
Santa Fe Railroad, 44, 45
Sarcobatus Flat, 86, 87
Schools
  in Amargosa Valley (1960s), 104
  in Clay Camp, 61-62
Selbach family, 101
  in Farm Area, 80
Sevier River, 49
Shoal Creek, 12
Shoshone (CA), 53
Shoshone indians. *See* Indians, Western Shoshone
Sierra Club, 96. *See also* Environmental movement
Silver
  in Panamint Mountains, 18. *See also* Lost Gunsight Lode
Silver Peak (NV), 21, 23
Sixmile Spring, 35
Smith, F. M. (Borax)
  borax discoveries, 41-42
  Pacific Coast Borax Company, 42
  and T&T Railroad, 42, 43-44, 50
Smith, Jedediah
  expeditions (1826-1827), 9
Smith, Orson K. (Capt.), 11, 12
  wagon party, 11-12, 13
Smith, Tracey W. *See* Boyd, Betty-Jo
Sodaville (NV), 75-76
Softball, 103-104. *See also* AVIA
Southern California Edison, 85, 68, 87. *See also* Electricity, in Amargosa Valley
Spanish Trail. *See* Old Spanish Trail
Spector Range, 98
Spiller, Henry, 38-39
SP, LA&SL. *See* San Pedro, Los Angeles, and Salt Lake Railroad
Spring Meadows, Inc.

purchase of Ash Meadows land, 93-94
Spring Meadows Ranch, 94, 95
Spring Mountains, 5, 6, 16, 24, 86
Staley homestead, 72
Stateline Saloon, 92, 102, 105-106
Stateline Trailer Park, 92
Steward, Julian, 1-2
Stewart Valley, 35
Sticht, Francis D'Albertin
  and Ash Meadows Lodge, 72
Stone House, 33, 34
Stretch, R. H., 21, 22-24
Strickland family
  in Farm Area, 80
Stump Spring, 16, 20
Sylvania (NV), 30
Sylvania Mountains, 30

T&T. *See* Tonopah and Tidewater Railroad
T&T Ranch, 67-68, 69, 75, 76, 80.
  See also under Bettles, Billie; Bettles, Gordon; Boyd, Betty-Jo; Records, H. H. "Hank"
Tecopa (CA), 11, 20, 45, 76
Teel's Marsh (NV), 41
Telescope Range, 24
Tenneco (company), 91, 92
Test Site. *See* Nevada Test Site
Thomas, William H. (sheriff), 87-88
Thurman, Slim, 105
Timpahute (NV), 27
Toiyabe Range, 18
Toles, Herb, 70, 71
Tonopah (NV), 31-32, 42, 46
Tonopah and Tidewater Railroad (T&T), 42, 43-45, 50, 58, 65, 71, 75
  development of farm at Leeland Station, 67-70
  section hands, 66
  stops in the 1920s-1930s, 65-67, 70, 73

Tourism, 109
Towne Pass, 17
Towner, Charles W., 26
Travertine Springs, 13
Truman, Harry, 95, 98
Tubbs family, 72, 101

United Death Valley Clay, 59, 60
U.S. Fish and Wildlife Service, 95,
    96
U.S. Supreme Court
    decision on Devils Hole pupfish
        (1976), 95

Valley Crest Park (CA), 92
Vanderbilt Mine (clay), 91. *See also*
    Clay
Volcano Wash, 35, 36
von Schmidt, Alexis, 19

Wade, Harry, 12, 17
Wagner, Gordon, 101
Wagon parties. *See* Bennett-Arcan
    wagon party; Hunt, Jefferson,
    wagon party; Smith, Orson K.,
    wagon party
Walkara (Ute), 10, 11
Water, 2, 68, 83
    in Ash Meadows, 14, 15, 25, 33-
        34, 67, 109
    in Devils Hole, 95
    state attempts to restrict usage,
        83-84
    See also Amargosa Valley,

geography/topography;
    Wells
Wells
    in Ash Meadows, 94
    in Farm Area, 3, 67, 81
    on T&T Ranch, 69, 79, 84
    See also Water
Wheeler, George M. (Lt.)
    geological surveys, 21, 28
Wildlife conservation. *See* Environ-
    mental movement
Williams, Walt, 85
Windsor, Jessie
    and Ash Meadows Lodge, 72
Winters, Aaron, 36
    borax discovery, 38-39
    home at Ash Meadows, 37-38
Winters, Rosie, 36, 39
    home at Ash Meadows, 37-38
Winters' Hole, 36
Women, in Amargosa Valley
    (early years), 83

York, Fran, 105
Yount, Joseph, 26
Yount family, 26
Yucca Mountain, 16
    nuclear waste repository, 110

Zabriskie, C. B., 68
Zabriskie Point, 68
Zanjani, Sally (*Jack Longstreet: Last
    of the Desert Frontiersmen*), 30,
    32

Books from Nye County Press
by Robert D. McCracken

A History of Amargosa Valley, Nevada (cloth)
ISBN: 1-878138-56-1

The Modern Pioneers of the Amargosa Valley (paper)
ISBN: 1-878138-58-8

A History of Beatty, Nevada (cloth)
ISBN: 1-878138-54-5

Beatty: The Town that Survived and Grew (paper)
ISBN: 1-878138-55-3

A History of Pahrump, Nevada (cloth)
ISBN: 1-878138-51-0

Pahrump: A Valley Waiting to Become a City (paper)
ISBN: 1-878138-53-7

A History of Tonopah, Nevada (cloth)
ISBN: 1-878138-52-9

*Tonopah: The Greatest, the Richest, and the Best Mining Town
in the World* (paper)
ISBN: 1-878138-50-2

 Nye County Press
P.O. Box 3070
Tonopah, NV 89049